What You Knead

What You Knead

■

Mary Ann Esposito

Photographs by Bill Truslow

William Morrow and Company, Inc.
New York

It is the policy of William Morrow and Company, Inc., and its imprints and
affiliates, recognizing the importance of preserving what has been written, to
print the books we publish on acid-free paper, and we exert our best efforts
to that end.

Library of Congress Cataloging-in-Publication Data

Esposito, Mary Ann.
What you knead/by Mary Ann Esposito.
p. cm.
Includes index.
ISBN 0-688-15010-1
1. Dough. I. Title.
TX769.E87 1997
641.8'15—dc21 97-11279

Printed in the United States of America

First Edition

1 2 3 4 5 6 7 8 9 10

BOOK DESIGN BY RICHARD ORIOLO

For Leslie, Cynthia, Donna, Connie, Ruth, Jan, and Liz, whose
unconditional friendship is one of my great treasures

Preface

■

What You Knead is a perfect title for this wonderful book, which will guide you clearly into the delightful and rewarding world of scratch bread baking. Like many "simple" endeavors, the joy of baking bread from "scratch" endures and improves with age. After only a few tries, this will become second nature to you. You will memorize the recipe and incorporate the technique into your being forever. By then you will also have added your personal touch which will distinguish your bread from all others. Yes, bread baking is an art!

Anyone who has met or watched Mary Ann knows one couldn't ask for a better master teacher. Her knowledge, enthusiasm, and warmth are legendary. They certainly flow into this book. You will be attracted and inspired by her characteristic love for what she is doing and sharing. It is contagious and empowering.

When I entered our flour business some four decades ago by selling flour to Boston area retail and wholesale bakers, I was intrigued by what inspired/drove these people to begin a twelve-hour workday in the wee hours of the morning, usually six and sometimes seven days a week. My conclusion is that there is something unique and even mystical about beginning each workday with pure, simple, basic ingredients and creating virtual art which one can see, feel, smell, and taste by the end of the day. Quite simply, it is nourishment for the soul as well as the body.

Mary Ann knows this, breathes this, and, fortunately for the rest of us, shares it with her characteristic expertise and caring.

Frank Sands, President
King Arthur Flour Company

Acknowledgments

■

I have always wanted to write a book about how to make and work with simple yeast dough, but I did not realize how much time I would have to spend with my hands in dough. After a year and a half spent measuring two hundred pounds of flour and kneading tubfuls of dough in order to test the recipes, I finally dusted the flour from my hands and thought that my job was done. Little did I realize what was still to come. Words on a page describing recipes and instructing one how to use them are one thing, but to make this book truly come alive (as yeast does when it is combined with water and flour), and to make it as personal a bread-baking adventure for you as possible, I literally went through a déjà vu experience, making many of the recipes again with a team of dedicated bakers in order to create the technique photographs for this book. I hope these will help to guide your hands, no matter how experienced or inexperienced you are with yeast doughs. In addition, there are wonderful eat-off-the-pages "beauty shots" that tell the story of the finished products.

These photographs, and the organization of the book, are the work of a talented group of people, all of whom are special to me and are *buono, come il pane,* "as good as bread," a charming Italian phrase that has come to mean that one is much respected and held in high regard. It seems a fitting way for me to say thank you to the many people who have put so much of their vision and spirit into this book.

To my initial editor, Ann Bramson, for her enthusiasm for this project—which grew like a bowl of rising dough—her critical, artistic eye set this book apart and gave it its user-friendly appeal; and to my editor, Pam Hoenig, who gave the final shaping to the book and took this project to completion. To David Nussbaum, the project coordinator for the book shoot, for his dedication and determination to get everything right; he kept our photography and kitchen crews on track, and his proofing box was always filled with the "next dough to go." To photographer Bill Truslow, a longtime friend who has worked on all my books, for his never-waning enthusiasm at working together once again, and for his energy and ability to capture the story and essence of each dough product. To the team at William Morrow, who collectively gave this book its polished look: Richard Aquan, for the stunning book jacket design; Richard Oriolo, for the interior design; Jennifer Kaye, for always having answers to my questions; and Deborah Weiss-Geline, chief copyeditor, Judith Sutton, copyeditor, Ann Cahn, production editor, and Karen Lumley, production manager, for making the written word come together. To Al Marchioni, for his direction over the years and for his many kindnesses and genuine interest in all of my books. To Paul Fedorko, for smoothing the transition. To Carrie Weinberg, for getting the word out that I was baking, and for directing a polished book tour. To Trish Dahl, food stylist, for her enduring patience and talent for capturing the reality of each bread product and allowing it to speak to the camera. To Jane Sutton, prop stylist, for her fresh ideas in telling the story of each recipe. To Liz Hayden, one of the culinary supervisors of my PBS series *Ciao Italia*, for her dependability and ability to knead dough into the wee hours, always with a smile. To Andrea Chatis and Andrew Steere, for making the long baking days run smoothly— they did everything from wash dishes to provide lunch for the entire book crew. To City & Country, and John Seath and Glenn Gerace, for their generosity once again in the lending of beautiful dishes and serving pieces. To Anne Clune, of Sunflours Bakery, for the loan of antique props and to Anichini Inc., for the loan of their exquisite Italian linens for the beauty shots and book jacket photograph. To my agent, Michael Jones, for his vision in helping me set attainable goals, and to my family: my husband, Guy, who is an accomplished bread baker in his own right, and my children, Beth and Chris, who are finally making their own bread.

Contents

∎

Nonna's Sponge Dough

Simply Sweet Dough

Beyond Bread Crumbs

Homemade Is Better

Introduction

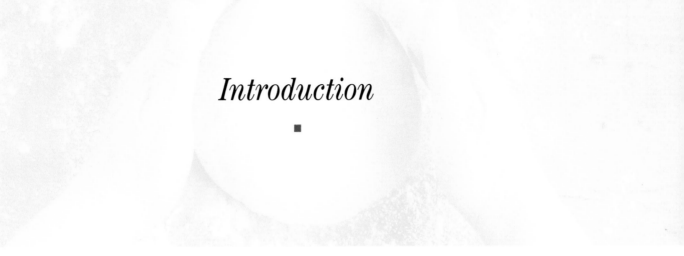

"I am afraid to work with yeast." So many people said this to me that it became a pleasurable mission of mine to help them see how easy it is to make simple yeast dough.

This book offers you, the home baker, three basic doughs, all of which begin life in the same way, with water, yeast, and flour. These ingredients become the foundation for the Straight Dough, Nonna's Sponge Dough, and Simply Sweet Dough.

I wanted to present you with a book that was simple to use but offered a variety of wonderful possibilities. Each of these doughs can be turned into dozens of different baked goods—and, in effect, change personalities with the addition of a few ingredients.

The book's first chapter introduces you to easy-to-make Straight Dough that, among other possibilities, can be shaped into a homey loaf of country bread, Pane Casereccio, become the casing for an elegant Italian chicken pie, or serve as the envelope for double-crusted roasted pepper focaccia. But don't stop there: With a few additional ingredients, the dough easily changes character.

Nonna's Sponge Dough is my Grandmother Galasso's recipe. This clever dough begins with a *madre*—a mother dough, also called a sponge. It was just a little potato water left over from boiling potatoes combined with yeast and flour and left to rise for a few hours before more flour and water were added to it. Grandma claimed that the *madre* gave dough *forza* (strength) and she was right! The whole idea of using a sponge is to provide additional strength and character to dough. This dough is like Joseph's kaleidoscopic dream coat of many colors: Fashion it into a variety of breads, each with its own look; change the taste with a few added ingredients; and create your own "dough of many colors" with the variations suggested in the recipes. Some of my favorites are a chewy raisin and molasses bread, a tangy dried-tomato pesto and black olive pizza, and plump calzones filled with roasted vegetables, which make welcome snacks or lunch box and picnic food.

If you love sweet yeast dough, Simply Sweet Dough is for you. Enriched with eggs, butter, sugar, and flavorings, this dough can become coiled little sweet rolls that form a wreath or delicate donuts oozing with velvety pastry cream, reminiscent of those found in Tuscany. There are charming holiday breads too, made memorable with the addition of almond paste. Or, for something just a little different, make the ice cream cones that can be filled with pastry cream, sorbet, mousses, and of course ice cream.

And leftover bread is not left out of this book. It can wear a new coat too: Turn it into a cool marinated summer salad or a comforting bread pudding.

For me, there is nothing like my own pair of hands when it comes to making dough. Call me old-fashioned, but the time-honored tradition of hand-working dough puts me in tune with the whole process of making bread. It is with my hands that I, the baker, am drawn to and connected with this ancient craft. Only my hands "know" the right consistency of dough, only hand kneading can impart a unique character to dough, and only hand shaping can create the dough's individuality. And who among bakers, whether amateur or professional, has not experienced the satisfaction that comes from announcing, "I made it by hand."

This is not to say that I don't have some equipment in my kitchen to speed the process occasionally, like a heavy-duty mixer and a food processor, but I have pulled the plug on bread machines. I admit that bread made with a bread machine is far more appealing than the mass-produced so-called bread in a cellophane wrapper. But a bread machine is just that . . . a machine, devoid of human involvement.

I learned to make yeast dough at home watching my Italian grandmother and mother make our daily bread. Sacks of flour, most of them Canadian, were kept stored in the cold back room near the kitchen. For my grandmother and mother, Canadian flour was prized for its superior quality, because it was milled from hard wheat, a high gluten flour that gave it the power to turn out a good sturdy loaf of bread. Each day, mounds of this flour appeared on my mother's worn wooden counter. Since Nonna Galasso lived with us, the dough was always made the way it was done in her home province of Avellino, Italy. First the flour was fashioned into an imposing round wall affectionately called *la fontana* (the fountain). In the middle of the fontana was a large pool of warm water. I watched in fascination as small, square, moist yeast cakes were carefully crumbled between my grandmother's fingers into the water. To my impressionable eye, the whole scene resembled a lake surrounded by soft mountain peaks. The only things rippling the water were the experienced hands of my grandmother, or mother, working the flour so fast into the center that watching the process seemed like looking at a blurred photograph.

Enormous yellow and green spongeware bowls cradled the dough after it was mixed. As it rose in a warm spot near the stove, covered in heavy blankets, the urge sometimes rose in me to drive my fist right into the center of that nearly exploding mass and watch it fall like a deflating balloon. I did not know then that carbon dioxide gas forming in the fermenting dough caused it to rise. I only knew grandma's intuitive explanation, "*la pasta cresce*"—the dough had woken up from its sleep and was growing.

Now, years later, making bread dough is still my favorite baking activity but I have a much deeper understanding of the basic ingredients and how they work in combination to produce good dough. From my grandmother's adopted American kitchen to the kitchens of Italy, I have watched Italian bakers create all sorts of yeasted breads, rolls, pizze, and focaccia. I have listened to their explanations of how to make the best dough, their comments often humanizing the dough itself as they determined whether it was too thirsty or not thirsty, whether it was too cold or too warm, and whether it was sleeping or not. In each instance, a deep reverence for the basic ingredients prevailed.

When I walk into a *panificio* (bread bakery) in Italy, the pride in workmanship is evident for all to see, smell, taste, and marvel at. On display are bursting crusty brown breads of every shape and size, the colorful canvases of pizze, fragrant focaccia, and knotty-looking breadsticks, all of which have come from the mouth of gigantic stone ovens. All of these breads enjoy a very short shelf life as people eagerly come to purchase them almost as soon as they are scooped from the oven floor. Nowhere is this enthusiasm more in evidence than in Sicily, which in antiquity was the original breadbasket of Italy. In the little town of Vallelunga, the Il Forno (the oven) bakery cannot turn out breads and pizze fast enough for all of its customers. Fuzze, the baker, and his family take great pride in making *pane Siciliano,* the typical golden-grained semolina bread of the island, and the intensely flavored *sfincione,* Sicilian pizza glistening with a cover of deep red plum tomato sauce, silvery oil-packed sardines, pungent black olives, and a thin veil of grated Pecorino sheep's milk cheese topping it all. This is honest hand-fashioned food at its very best, both for those who make it and for those who enjoy it.

I wish you the same kind of satisfaction with the three master dough recipes in this book. Making a simple dough from water, yeast, and flour not only creates food to satisfy a basic hunger, it also perpetuates one of the world's oldest culinary traditions. *Buon divertimento!*

Note: Most of the recipes in this book have a decidedly Italian style and flavor. That is as it should be, for it is nearly impossible to move too far from one's roots.

What You Knead

The Baker's Pantry

■

Most cooks have a place in their kitchen called the pantry. Whether it is a small cupboard, replenished frequently, or a walk-in room, where the choices are as varied as the foods lining a supermarket aisle, a pantry is the soul of the kitchen and fires our imagination with ways to cook our favorite foods. When I walk into my pantry, I see before me shelves of dormant ingredients that dare me to be creative, and I realize that with a shake of this and a sprinkle of that, foods can surprise us in unexpected ways.

Basic Ingredients

The old adage that it is "quality rather than quantity that matters" is certainly true when it comes to stocking the right ingredients in your pantry for yeast dough baking. Although the basic list is not long, paying attention to details will save you time in the kitchen and make all the difference. If you were to walk into my pantry or peek into my refrigerator, here is what you would find.

Baking sprays: I use olive oil and vegetable oil baking sprays to coat bowls for rising dough, to coat plastic bags for storing dough in the refrigerator or freezer, and to coat baking sheets.

Butter: I like using unsalted butter because it is fresher and sweeter tasting than salted butter.

Candied citrus peels: I use diced sugar-coated lemon or orange peels in many of my recipes for sweet breads. I like to make my own candied orange and lemon peel (see page 135), but you can use commercially prepared peel.

Citron: The peel of this pale green fruit belonging to the citrus family is candied and used in Italian breads and cakes such as panettone and panforte. It is easy to find around holiday time, and that is the time to stock up. It will last for months in your refrigerator.

Eggs: Purchasing eggs requires close inspection. Look for eggs with no hairline cracks. Store eggs in their cartons on one of the shelves of your refrigerator, not in compartments in the refrigerator door, which are not cold enough. The recipes in this book call for large eggs. It makes no difference if you use brown or white eggs.

Extracts: Buy pure natural extracts and flavorings. These are made from neutral grain alcohol; a pure extract must contain 35 percent alcohol. Vanilla, the most commonly used extract, comes from the vanilla bean, the seedpod of a tropical climbing orchid. Other popular extracts are almond, orange, and rum. (See the recipe on page 136 to make your own vanilla extract, or Mail-Order Sources, page 143, for purchasing pure extracts of all types.)

Flour: The three master doughs in this book call for only one flour, an unbleached all-purpose hard-wheat flour high enough in gluten to give the proper structure to the dough and to allow the risen dough to be kneaded easily. A hard winter wheat flour with a protein content of between 11 and 12 percent is best (see Mail-Order Sources, page 143). All the recipes in this book were tested with King Arthur unbleached all-purpose flour.

Fruits: Dried fruits are an integral part of some of the recipes in this book. Sometimes I cook them as fillings for rolls and breads, other times I soak them in liqueur before kneading them into dough. Always buy unsulphured fruits. Those I use most often are (California) apricots, prunes, pears, apples, peaches, cherries, cranberries, and raisins.

Honey: This natural sweetener (derived by bees from flower pollen) is a combination of fructose, glucose, and water. It belongs in every baker's pantry. It can be used in place of granulated sugar in many recipes—and in fact you will need to use less honey than sugar for the same sweetness—and it adds its own unique flavor to many sweet breads and other baked goods.

Milk: I prefer to use 1 percent low-fat milk for yeast doughs because it does not impede the activity of dried yeast as much as full-fat whole milk (fat slows the activity of yeast).

Molasses: Without molasses, the Country Raisin Molasses Bread on page 72 would not have its special flavor and character. Molasses is the syrup that is left after making refined white sugar from sugarcane and beets. Buy unsulphured molasses, which means that sulphur dioxide was not used to clarify the molasses in processing.

Nuts: Almonds, hazelnuts, walnuts, and pignoli (pine nuts) are always in my kitchen. I store them in jars in the refrigerator to ensure freshness. To enhance the flavor of nuts, toast them first in the oven or in a dry skillet before adding them to recipes.

Olive oil: Olive oil is important in all my cooking and baking. I always use fruity extra-virgin olive oil; this is olive oil that has less than 1 percent acidity and was cold pressed, rather than chemically extracted or treated with heat.

Salt: The use of salt in recipes is a matter of personal choice. I like to use fine or coarse sea salt for its natural taste. Unlike table salt, sea salt contains trace minerals that have not been destroyed by chemical processing. It has a stronger flavor than regular table salt, so you can use less of it.

Seeds: My refrigerator is home to jars of poppy, sesame, and sunflower seeds. Refrigeration helps to prevent seeds, especially oilier ones like these, from becoming rancid.

Spices: Any baker should have fragrant spices such as cinnamon, cloves, nutmeg, mace, allspice, and ginger on hand. Keep spices in well-sealed containers in a dark, cool place, and replace them every six months.

Sugars: Brown, confectioners', granulated, and turbinado sugars all have their purpose in my kitchen.

- Brown sugar is a mixture of refined white sugar and molasses.

- Confectioners' sugar is a powdered refined white sugar with some cornstarch added to prevent clumping. I like to dust it over the top of plump Plum Kuchen (page 109) or use it to make a glaze to drizzle over Fig, Chocolate, and Walnut Braid (page 97).

- Turbinado sugar is coarse light brown sugar. It does not dissolve or melt in the oven's heat as readily as granulated sugar. I sprinkle it on Sweet Spiral Wreath (page 113) and Ciambella (page 95) for added crunch.

Water: Bakers in different cities can make the same dough, following the instructions exactly, even using the same type of flour and yeast, but their breads will be different because the quality of tap water in their respective locales will affect the final product both in taste and in look. I recommend noncarbonated filtered or bottled water for the recipes in this book.

Yeast: The recipes in this book have been tested with either Fleischmann's or Red Star active dry yeast. Both are reliable products readily available in supermarkets. I don't use rapid-rise yeast, because I prefer a slow fermentation of the dough to allow it to develop a good flavor. Although the yeast we had at home when I was growing up was always fresh cakes of yeast, I haven't used it in any of the recipes in this book because it has a shorter shelf life than dried yeast.

A package of active dry yeast weighs 1/4 ounce and contains 2 1/4 teaspoons dried yeast granules. When purchasing active dry yeast, be sure to check the expiration date on the package.

Zest: Grating the skins of citrus fruits such as lemons and oranges produces flavorful zests that can add intense flavors to foods. Orange zest is particularly good in Poppy Seed Pretzels (page 99), and the lemon zest in the Fratti di Lucca (page 31) will entice you to try more than one. I like to grate enough fruit zest to freeze in small plastic bags so it is always on hand.

Basic Equipment

Over the years, I have gathered certain necessary and favorite tools of the trade that are helpful when working with dough. Here is my basic checklist.

Baker's peel: Among my most treasured bread-making tools are several long-handled wooden paddles upon which dough is placed after it is shaped for the final rise. The dough is then slid from the peel onto a preheated baking stone to bake.

Baking sheets: I have baking sheets in various sizes. I like heavy nonstick types for their convenience, as well as the heavy-duty double-insulated and rimless sheets.

Baking stone: A baking stone is the sure way to get crusty evenly browned and baked loaves of bread. These unglazed stones may be round, square, or rectangular. Put the stone on the bottom rack of the oven to preheat before placing the risen dough on it to bake. The stone conducts heat evenly and helps the dough to form a crisp bottom crust and an even color.

Banneton: If you want a bread with a nice appearance, let the dough have its final rise in a cloth-lined woven willow basket called a banneton. The dough takes on the shape and design of the basket. When it is ready to bake, it is carefully turned out of the basket onto a hot baking stone or a baking sheet.

Bench knife: When I am kneading dough I often use this handy tool, which is sometimes referred to as a dough scraper, to help lift and turn the dough. Use it to scrape bits of dough off your work surface as well as to divide dough into smaller pieces.

Bread bowls: You can never have too many mixing and rising bowls. Clear glass or ceramic bowls in assorted sizes are handy, and several four- and five-quart bowls are indispensable when you work with a lot of flour.

Bread knife: If you want to cut neat slices of bread, you need a knife blade with a serrated edge that saws through rather than tears bread.

Charlotte mold: Of all the types of molds I have, the one that gets the most use is the charlotte mold. This is a deep pan with slightly sloping sides and two handles. Charlotte molds come in various sizes; mine is 4 inches high by 6 inches wide. I use it for making the Almost Apple Charlotte on page 91. Use these molds for yeasted coffee cakes and holiday breads as well.

Cooling racks: Large wire racks allow air to circulate around just-baked bread so the underside does not get soft.

Food processor: One of the most useful pieces of equipment in my kitchen is a commercial-size food processor. It is great for pureeing fillings and chopping nuts. Occasionally I use the dough blade for speeding the process of making dough when I'm dealing with large amounts of ingredients.

Jelly-roll pan: This baking sheet, measuring 10 by 15 by 3/4 to 1 inch is just the thing to hold a large shaped bread. Heavy stainless steel sheets are the best.

Heavy-duty stand mixer: In addition to a whisk beater, this mixer comes with a dough hook and a paddle or batter blade, both of which are useful when mixing a large batch of dough. I use it for making the Country Raisin Molasses Bread on page 72.

Instant-read thermometer: No bread baker's kitchen should be without this indispensable tool. I use it for gauging the correct temperature of liquids for proofing yeast, as well as for determining whether the temperature of rising dough is what it should be.

Lame: This small French tool is basically a razor blade set into a handle. It is used to slash or score the tops of loaves before baking to allow the carbon dioxide gases to escape without splitting the bread.

Measuring cups: Every kitchen needs both a set of heavy-duty stainless steel dry measures and a set of liquid measures. It's handy to have more than one set.

Measuring spoons: Heavy-duty stainless steel measuring spoons are more accurate and sturdier than plastic or flimsy metal spoons.

Parchment paper: I am partial to using nonstick parchment paper or baking parchment to line peels. It allows dough to slide easily from peel to stone, and there is no cleanup.

Pastry brushes: I like good natural-bristle brushes in assorted sizes for brushing the tops of doughs with water or egg washes. Use them to lightly grease baking pans.

Pastry wheel: This small cutting tool has a sharp metal cutting wheel, either plain or fluted, and a sturdy wooden handle. I have a collection of these; I use one with a fluted wheel for cutting decorative zigzag lattice strips for pies and braided loaves.

Pizza pans: Perforated 16- to 18-inch-diameter heavy-duty aluminum pizza pans are perfect for allowing even heat distribution so bottom crusts can crisp. They are a good choice if you do not use a stone to bake pizza. Nonperforated pans (13 to 14 inches in diameter) are also available.

Plastic wrap: The best thing to use to cover a bowl of rising dough is plastic wrap. Tightly fitted over the bowl, it helps trap both heat and gas for a better rise.

Rolling pins: I love the control that long narrow wooden handleless Italian-style rolling pins give me when working with dough.

Scale: For foolproof baking, one of the pieces of equipment a serious baker must have is a scale for weighing ingredients. I prefer the digital types that give weights in grams and ounces.

Spatulas: Keep an assortment of sturdy spatulas with wooden handles and heavy rubber blades in assorted sizes, from 1¼ to 4½ inches wide. Wide-bladed stainless steel spatulas are great for lifting large breads off baking sheets.

Spritzer bottle: I use a mister to spray my oven walls with water just after putting the dough in to bake, and then a few times during the first ten minutes or so of baking. The steam that is created helps the bread develop a crisp crust.

Timer: It's easy to keep track of proofing, rising, and baking times with a timer. Some of the digital types can be set for three different times.

Bread-Making Basics

■

What You Need to Know

The first thing I do when I make a basic yeast dough is assemble all the ingredients. First I reach for unbleached all-purpose flour made from hard wheat. Hard wheat flour has a protein content between 11 and 12 percent and contains enough gluten to allow for easy rolling and stretching of dough. It also gives bread the proper structure, and gives it character as well. I always keep flour in tightly closed containers in my refrigerator and bring the flour to room temperature before I want to use it.

Measuring Flour

I measure flour either by weighing it on a scale or by using the sprinkle and sweep method. Most professional bakers, especially European bakers, always weigh flour and other ingredients for baking. Home bakers do not tend to weigh ingredients, preferring instead to dip a measuring cup directly into the container of flour. And that is where trouble begins. A cup of flour can weigh between 3.5 and 6 ounces, depending on the way you measure it. Properly measured, without packing it, a cup of flour by weight should average between 3.5 and 4 ounces; in these recipes, a cup of flour equals

Measuring Flour

Weighing flour on a scale

Spooning the flour into the measure, using the sprinkle and sweep method

Proofing Yeast

Add yeast to warm water

Stirring yeast in the water

The proofed yeast

3.5 ounces. Dipping a measuring cup into a bag of flour, however, immediately compacts the flour and gives you more than you want (as much as 5 to 6 ounces). The end result will be a dry, unknead-able dough and a baked loaf as heavy as a rock, with a tight exterior texture or crumb and floury taste. Investing in a kitchen scale will enable you to avoid this and give you baking accuracy, but if you do not have a scale, use the sprinkle and sweep method.

The sprinkle and sweep method

Hold a measuring cup over the flour bag or storage container and with a large spoon, sprinkle the flour into the cup until it overflows the cup. With a butter knife or other straight edge, sweep the excess flour from the top of the cup. Place the measured flour in a bowl or heap it on your work surface. Working with a heap of flour is the way I like to make yeast dough because I grew up learn-ing that method. At home, it was reverently called *la fontana* (the fountain), and it was the same method my mother and grandmother used to make fresh pasta.

Working with Yeast

Now that we have the flour measured and waiting, what about the yeast and water? Active dry yeast is used in all of the recipes in this book. It is easier to use than fresh cake yeast and has a longer shelf life, so it can be bought in bulk and stored in the refrigerator or freezer. Do not use fast-rising or instant dried yeast; these were developed for people in a hurry, who, in my opinion, do not want to have fun in the kitchen. Quick-rising or instant yeast will produce an entirely different taste, one that is not as fully developed as dough made with regular active dry yeast.

To activate yeast, it must be dissolved in warm water, water that is between 100° and 115°F. If the water is too hot, it can kill the yeast. If it's too cool, the yeast will not activate at all, or it will take a long time to do so. How are you going to be sure of the water temperature? Invest in an instant-read thermometer, found in any hardware store. The thermometer is also handy for check-ing the temperature of dough as it is rising and will give you an accurate indication of when bread is fully baked.

Now we can turn our attention to the water. Believe it or not, the purity of the water used to make dough will make a tremendous difference in the taste of the bread. Most tap water is heav-ily chlorinated, and this chemical taste is transferred to the dough. Instead, I use noncarbonated fil-tered or bottled water.

Mixing the Dough

The first step in mixing the dough is proofing the yeast. This simply means activating the yeast so it can do its job. Pour the amount of warm water indicated in the recipe for dissolving the yeast into a large bowl and sprinkle the yeast over the top. Stir the yeast with a spoon or your fingers. Let the

The Fontana Method

Forming the fontana

Adding water and yeast
to the fontana

Incorporating the flour
in the liquid

Lifting and turning the dough
with the bench knife

Ball of dough ready
for kneading

yeast proof for about 5 minutes. You will notice chalky-looking bubbles beginning to appear on the surface of the water. This indicates that the yeast is ready to do its work. (If the yeast does not bubble at all, it is old and you will have to start over.) Stir in the remaining amount of water called for in the recipe.

Now it is time to add the flour and salt. Add the flour gradually to allow it to absorb the water slowly. You may not need all the flour called for in a recipe, or you may need additional flour; most of the recipes in this book give a range for flour. There are many factors determining the amount of flour required, including the type of flour used, the way it was measured, and the humidity in the air. As you become familiar with making dough, your hands will tell you "by feel" when the right amount of flour has been added.

Salt is an important addition to dough. It helps to control the rate of fermentation in the dough, and thus allows the dough to develop its flavor slowly. Add the salt after you have added and mixed in half of the flour into the yeast mixture.

With the basic ingredients of water, yeast, flour, and salt at hand, we are now ready to make a basic dough, and there are two methods that I like. One is to make the dough using the traditional method, the fontana, and the other is to make it in a bowl.

To make the dough using the fontana method

Heap the flour onto a work surface and sprinkle the salt over it. Make a hole in the center of the flour with your hand. Proof the yeast in the amount of water indicated in the recipe in a 2- to 4-cup capacity measuring cup or in a medium size bowl. Add the remaining water called for in the recipe to the proofed yeast, stir well, then pour the liquid into the center of the fontana. Now begin bringing the flour into the water from the inside wall of the fontana, moving your fingers clockwise as you incorporate the flour. Be careful not to break through the wall—but if you do, catch the water with some of the flour. I usually use one hand to work in the flour and keep the other hand on the outside of the wall just in case the wall breaks. As you work, the flour and water mixture will become thick and the wall of flour thinner. Now use your hands to bring in the remaining flour, using only enough to form a ball of dough. You may not need all the flour. Use a bench knife (dough scraper) to help you lift and turn the dough. The bench knife is also useful for pushing aside the excess flour, which can be sifted and recycled to sprinkle on your work surface for kneading. Use it to scrape up and remove any bits of hardened flour that are sticking to the work surface. Now you can begin to knead the dough on the work surface as described below.

To make the dough in a bowl

Gradually add the flour one cup at a time to the proofed yeast and water mixture, stirring in each addition with your hands or a wooden spoon. Once you have added about three quarters of the flour, add the salt. At some point, you will have to put down the spoon, if you're using it, and use your hands to finish mixing the dough. When you have added enough flour, the mixture should look like a shaggy mass. Turn the dough out on a floured work surface and begin to knead.

Mixing in a Bowl

Pouring the proofed yeast into the bowl

Adding flour to the yeast mixture

Mixing liquid and flour
together

Turning shaggy mass onto
work surface

Forming dough into ball

Kneading

| Grasp and turn dough | Fold the dough | Push and knead dough |

Kneading

Kneading the dough means pushing on the dough with the palms and heels of your hands, and turning and stretching it to develop the gluten. Kneading is important for a smooth, soft, and satiny dough, and it also helps to define the texture of the baked bread.

Kneading makes the dough elastic and smooth, evenly distributing the gases and yeast cells in the dough. I tend to knead with one hand initially until I have a barely sticky ball, then I finish kneading with two hands. As you knead, fold the dough over on itself, push the dough away from you, and fold it over again. Now give the dough a quarter turn to the right and continue the kneading action of folding, pushing, and turning. This will take about 5 minutes of work, but you will get into a rhythm and really be in tune with what you are doing. Use the bench knife to help you lift and turn the dough as you shape it into a ball. When it is fully kneaded, the dough will be soft, smooth, and no longer sticky.

The Rise

Use olive oil or vegetable oil spray to lightly coat a large bowl. Place the dough in the bowl and turn it to coat it with oil. Cover the bowl tightly with plastic wrap, place it in a warm but not too warm (77° to 80°F) spot, and allow it to double in size. For moist doughs, this will take about an

The Rise

Spraying bowl with
olive oil spray

Turning dough in bowl to
coat with olive oil

Covering the bowl tightly
with plastic wrap

Full risen dough

hour to an hour and a half. (Never place the dough in a preheated oven to rise. It will be too warm and will cause the dough to rise too quickly. You can, however, let it rise in a turned-off oven with a pilot light.) Use an instant-read thermometer to gauge the right temperature by inserting the thermometer into the center of the dough. From 77° to 80°F is an ideal temperature range. If the dough is too cool, move it to a warmer spot.

The rising action is caused by the action of the yeast, a living organism, feeding on the sugar and starches in the flour mixture, which results in the formation of carbon dioxide gas. The gas is trapped by the gluten strands in the dough and causes the dough to rise. As the dough rises, its flavor and texture begin to develop.

Check the rising dough after an hour or so. Is it ready to use? How do you know? First, look at it: It should have doubled in size. Smell it: It should smell yeasty. Then insert two fingers into the center. If the impression made does not close up, the dough is ready to punch down.

Deflating and Shaping

Punching down the dough deflates the trapped gases and evenly distributes the gluten in the dough, making it easier to knead. To deflate the dough, make a fist and gently push into the dough to collapse it. Now turn the dough out onto a lightly floured surface. Knead the dough for a good three to four minutes, using the fold, push, and turn method. Kneading the dough at this stage makes it smoother, gives it elasticity, and helps develop the gluten. As you knead, the dough will become easier to manipulate.

Now the dough can be shaped. Round, ring, long, and braided loaves are the most popular. See the photographs on pages 17–18 for these shaping techniques.

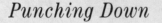
Punching Down

The deflated dough

Deflating the dough

Turning deflated dough onto
the work surface

Scoring Risen Loaf

Risen loaf ready
for scoring

Scoring the risen loaf

Second Rise

Once the dough has its final form, place it on a baking peel dusted with cornmeal or lined with parchment paper or on a baking sheet that has been lightly sprayed with olive oil or vegetable oil spray. Allow it to rise, covered with a clean cloth, until almost doubled in size again.

Baking

While the dough is rising, preheat the oven. If using a baking stone, put it on the lowest oven rack to preheat for at least 20 minutes.

Just before baking the bread, use a lame (see page 5), a clean razor blade, or small sharp knife to make several slashes in the top of the bread to allow steam and gases to escape while the bread is baking; the slashes prevent the bread from cracking open where you don't want it to. Slide the bread from the baker's peel onto the baking stone, along with the parchment paper. Or place the baking sheet on the lowest rack. Bake the bread according to the recipe directions.

To achieve a crisp crust, use a mister filled with water to spray the oven walls just after you put the bread in to bake. Mist the walls again a few times during the first 5 to 10 minutes or so of baking.

Fully baked bread is evenly browned on the top and bottom and sounds hollow when tapped on the bottom. To be absolutely sure, insert an instant-read thermometer into the center of the loaf. The temperature should be between 200° and 210°F.

Remove the bread to a cooling rack. Resist the temptation to cut into it immediately. Let the bread cool to room temperature, then use a serrated bread knife to cut it into slices.

Bread can be frozen successfully if tightly wrapped in heavy-duty foil, then sealed in a plastic bag. To defrost, remove the bread from its wrapping and thaw at room temperature. Reheat if desired.

Shaping the Loaves

Round Loaf

Pinching and tucking the loaf

Bottom of the pinched loaf

Forming the round

Ring Loaf

Swirling the center hole

Forming the hole
in the center

Forming the dough
into a round ring

Long Loaf

Forming the oval

Rolling the dough

Shaping the dough

Braided Loaf

Three strands of dough

Pinching the top of the
braid together

Forming the braid

Pinching and tucking in the ends

The Straight Dough

■

This chapter shows you how to make a simple straight-yeast dough that will become like a trusted friend—always predictable, dependable, and, most of all, adaptable. You may like this dough so much that you will find yourself wanting to experiment with it beyond the recipes in this chapter.

Fashion this dough into a simple loaf of bread, or use it as a container for a hearty chicken and vegetable pie; shape it into delicate dinner rolls, or make the irresistible chocolate-and-ricotta-filled Sicilian sweets called *iris*. These are but a few of the choices here.

The dough is called a straight dough because it doesn't use a sponge and because it is uncomplicated to put together, requiring just four ingredients: water, yeast, unbleached flour, and salt. The ingredients may be combined by hand, or in a heavy-duty mixer.

This dough can begin life in a *fontana* (fountain), using a traditional Italian hand-mixed method. The flour is measured directly onto the work surface and shaped into a mound with a hole in the center. The salt is sprinkled over the flour, then the liquid and other ingredients are poured into the hole and worked by hand to create a ball of dough. Less dramatic is putting the ingredients into a large bowl and combining them by hand. Both hand methods are illustrated with photographs on pages 10 and 12. Or you can make the dough in a heavy-duty mixer; see page 20 for directions.

Although I prefer to use this dough the day I make it, it can be made a day ahead. Allow it to rise once, then deflate it, place it in a plastic bag that has been coated with olive oil cooking spray, and refrigerate overnight. The next day, remove the dough from the bag, place it in a large bowl that has been sprayed with olive oil, and allow it to rise until almost doubled in size. (Or simply refrigerate it, tightly covered, in the bowl it rose in.) This may take a little longer than the time given in the recipe, because the dough is cold and will need additional time to come to room temperature.

If you want to make the dough and freeze it for future use, punch it down after the first rise, shape it into a ball, and place it in a plastic bag lightly sprayed with olive oil. Squeeze out any air in the bag, seal it tightly, and then seal it in another plastic bag. Freeze the dough for up to six months.

To use the frozen dough, remove it from the bag, and place it in a large bowl that has been lightly sprayed with olive oil. Cover the bowl tightly with plastic wrap and let the dough thaw, come to room temperature, and rise until almost doubled in size. Then use as directed in the individual recipe.

How to Make Simple Straight Dough in an Electric Mixer

I rarely use an electric mixer for making the Straight Dough, but each baker approaches tasks differently in the kitchen, so if you want to try making the dough in a mixer, here is how to do it.

My mixer is a heavy-duty KitchenAid stand mixer. It has a dough hook, batter paddle, and whisk attachment. I have found that the batter paddle actually works better at thoroughly mixing the dough than the dough hook, but you be the judge—try making dough with the dough hook and with the batter paddle, and see which you prefer.

Pour the amount of warm water indicated in the recipe for dissolving the yeast into the bowl of the mixer and sprinkle the yeast over the top. Attach the dough hook or batter paddle to the mixer and on low speed, mix the yeast into the water. Let the yeast proof for about 5 minutes, until the mixture has lots of chalky-looking bubbles on the top. Pour the remaining water into the bowl and stir on low speed to blend the yeast and water.

Add the flour 1 cup at a time, stirring on low speed to blend the ingredients. Add the salt with the third addition of flour. Turn the speed to medium-high and add just enough additional flour to create a dough that moves away from the sides of the bowl and clings to the dough hook or batter paddle. Stop the machine and feel the dough. It should be soft, but not sticky or gummy. If it is too sticky, add more flour, a tablespoon at a time, until the right consistency is obtained. If the dough is dry and crumbly, add a little water, about a teaspoon at a time, until the dough becomes soft and smooth.

Remove the bowl from the mixer base and turn the dough out onto a floured surface. With your hands, knead the dough for 3 to 4 minutes as described above, forming it into a ball. Lightly spray a large bowl with vegetable or olive oil spray and place the dough in the bowl. Turn the dough to coat with the oil, cover the bowl tightly with plastic wrap, and let the dough rise until doubled in size.

Straight Dough

■ MAKES 1 POUND, 14 OUNCES DOUGH

1 package active dry yeast (0.25 ounce)
1³/4 cups warm (110° to 115°F) filtered or
    bottled noncarbonated water
1 tablespoon extra-virgin olive oil
4 to 4¹/2 cups unbleached all-purpose flour
2 teaspoons fine sea salt

To make the dough using the fontana method, in a small bowl, dissolve the yeast in ¹/2 cup of the water, stirring to mix well. Let the yeast proof for about 5 minutes, or until tiny clusters of chalky-looking bubbles appear on the surface. Stir the remaining 1¹/4 cups water and the olive oil into the proofed yeast.

Mound the flour on a work surface and make a hole in the center of the flour (this is the fontana). Sprinkle the salt over the flour. Carefully pour the yeast mixture into the hole. Using your fingers, begin bringing the flour from the inside wall of the fontana into the liquid, working in a clockwise movement as you incorporate the flour. Be careful not to break through the wall; if any liquid does leak out, catch it with some of the flour. As you continue to incorporate the flour, a shaggy, lumpy mass will form; add just enough flour to make a dough that holds together. Push the excess flour to the side with a bench knife. Now you are ready to knead the dough: Knead until you have a soft ball of dough that is slightly tacky but not sticking to your hands, about 5 minutes. Lightly spray a large bowl with olive oil spray, put the dough in the bowl, and turn to coat it with oil. Cover the bowl tightly with plastic wrap and let the dough rise until almost doubled in size, about 1 hour.

To make the dough by hand in a bowl, dissolve the yeast in the water in a large bowl and proof as directed above, then add the remaining 1¹/4 cups water and the olive oil. Begin adding the flour to the yeast mixture, 1 cup at a time, mixing it in well with your hands. Add the salt with the third cup of flour. Add just enough flour so that the dough comes together in a shaggy mass. Turn the dough out onto a lightly floured surface and follow the directions above for kneading and rising.

To make the dough in an electric mixer, dissolve the yeast in the water in the mixer bowl and proof as directed above, then add the remaining 1¹/4 cups water and the olive oil. Follow the instructions on page 20 for mixing, kneading, and rising.

When the dough has risen and is almost doubled in size, it is ready to be used in any of the recipes in this chapter.

Pane Casereccio

The Straight Dough makes an honest and beautiful loaf of bread. When I was growing up, we called this *pane casereccio*, homemade bread, because we made it almost daily. I vary the free-form shape of the dough, making the classic round, long, ring, or braided shapes, then place it on a baker's peel to rise before slipping it into the oven onto a hot baking stone, but a baking sheet works fine too. ■ MAKES 1 LOAF

1 recipe Straight Dough (page 21)

Line a baker's peel with parchment paper or lightly spray a baking sheet with olive oil spray. Set aside.

Punch down the dough and turn it out onto a floured surface. Knead the dough for 3 to 4 minutes, until it is smooth and no longer sticky. Form the dough into a round, ring, long, or braided loaf (see pages 17–18) and place it on the baker's peel or baking sheet.

To make a braided loaf, divide the dough into thirds. Roll each piece into a 16- to 20-inch-long rope. Place the ropes side by side, leaving about 1 inch between them, on the baker's peel or baking sheet. Cross the top of the left rope over the middle rope. Cross the top of the right rope over the left rope. Pinch the ends together, then tuck them underneath the dough. Cross the middle rope over the left, cross the left rope over the right, and cross the right rope over the middle. Continue braiding to the ends of the ropes. Pinch the ends of the ropes together and tuck them underneath the loaf. Cover the dough with a clean cloth and let it rise until almost doubled in size.

Preheat the oven to 425°F if using a baking stone, or 400°F if baking the bread on a baking sheet. If using a stone, put it on the lowest oven rack to preheat.

If using a stone, hold the handle of the baker's peel and with a quick jerking motion, slide the dough, with the parchment paper, onto the baking stone. Using a mister, mist the oven walls with water and immediately close the oven door. Repeat the misting process two or three times more during the first 10 minutes of baking.

If using a baking sheet, put the bread in the oven on the sheet and mist the oven following the instructions above.

Bake the bread on the stone for 35 to 40 minutes, or on the sheet for 40 to 45 minutes, until it is evenly browned on the top and bottom and the bottom sounds hollow when tapped. Remove the bread to a cooling rack and let cool completely.

Braided Sesame Bread

Vary the flavors of these beautiful braided loaves by snipping some fresh herbs into the dough. Or add chopped tomatoes or olives, poppy seeds, or grated cheese, such as Parmigiano-Reggiano or Pecorino Romano. The possibilities are limited only by your imagination.

■ MAKES TWO 15½-INCH-LONG BRAIDED BREADS

1 recipe Straight Dough (page 21)
1 tablespoon extra-virgin olive oil
2 tablespoons sesame seeds
2 tablespoons coarse sea salt

Lightly spray two baking sheets with olive oil spray and set aside.

Punch down the dough and turn it out onto a lightly floured work surface. Knead the dough for 3 to 4 minutes, until smooth and no longer sticky.

Divide the dough into 6 equal pieces. Work with 3 pieces at a time, keeping the remaining pieces covered with a towel or bowl.

Roll each piece of dough back and forth under the palms of your hands into a 16-inch-long rope. Place the 3 ropes side by side on one of the baking sheets, leaving a 1-inch space between each one. Cross the top of the left rope over the middle rope and cross the top of the right rope over the left rope. Pinch the ends together and tuck them underneath the dough. Cross the middle rope over the left, cross the left rope over the right rope, and cross the right rope over the middle rope. Continue braiding to the ends of the ropes. Pinch the ends of the ropes together and tuck them underneath the loaf. Repeat the process with the remaining 3 pieces of dough.

Brush the braided loaves with the olive oil, then sprinkle the sesame seeds and coarse salt over the tops. Let the braids rise, covered with a towel, for 20 minutes.

Preheat the oven to 400°F.

Bake the braids for 30 to 35 minutes, until they are golden brown on the top and bottom and sound hollow when tapped on the bottom. Cool the braids on a rack before slicing.

Grissini Rustici/Country Breadsticks

When is a breadstick more than a breadstick? When it's a knotty, puffy, shiny, irregular-looking stick flavored with bits of prosciutto, sharp provolone cheese, and zucchini. These are great as an antipasto or a snack, or pack a handful for lunch instead of a sandwich! For a party, stand them up in a country crock. Or tie a bunch with a pretty ribbon and give as a gift from your kitchen.

■ MAKES 28 BREADSTICKS

6 ounces aged provolone cheese, minced
1/4 pound prosciutto, minced
1 small zucchini, minced
Fine sea salt to taste
1 recipe Straight Dough (page 21)
2 teaspoons extra-virgin olive oil
1 egg, slightly beaten

Preheat the oven to 375°F. Lightly grease four baking sheets with olive oil spray and set aside.

In a bowl, mix the cheese, prosciutto, zucchini, and salt together. Set aside.

Punch down the risen dough and turn it out onto a lightly floured surface. Knead the dough for 3 to 4 minutes, until smooth and no longer sticky.

Divide the dough in half. Work with one half at a time, keeping the remaining dough covered with a towel or bowl.

On the lightly floured surface, roll one piece of dough out into a rough circle about 14 inches in diameter. Brush the dough with 1 teaspoon of the olive oil. Spread half the filling ingredients evenly over the dough.

Starting from the edge nearest you, roll the dough up like a jelly roll, tucking in the ends as you roll to keep the filling from falling out. Pinch the seam closed.

Stretch the dough into a 14-inch log. Cut the log into 14 pieces with a bench scraper or knife.

On the floured surface, roll each piece under the palms of your hands into a 10-inch-long stick. Don't worry if some of the filling falls out—just press it back into the dough. Place the sticks on the prepared baking sheets, spacing them evenly. Brush the tops of the sticks with some of the beaten egg.

Bake for 20 to 25 minutes, until the breadsticks are golden brown and shiny. Remove the breadsticks to a cooling rack. Meanwhile, repeat the shaping process with the remaining dough, oil, and filling. When the first breadsticks are done, bake the second batch.

continued

The risen dough and filling ready to form the breadsticks

Spreading filling on
flat dough

Rolling filling inside dough

Pinching seam closed

Cutting dough into pieces

Rolling piece to form
breadstick

Formed breadsticks ready
for egg wash

Focaccia Doppia/Double-Crusted Focaccia

Focaccia doppia, an elegant-looking and unusual two-crusted pizza, can serve as a hearty antipasto for an informal dinner party or become the centerpiece for lunch or dinner with a salad.

The savory filling of grilled sweet red and yellow peppers and soppressata salami, spicy sausage seasoned with pepper and cloves, is best made a few hours ahead so the flavors can mingle. (Genoa salami, although milder in taste, can be substituted for the soppressata.) The focaccia can be assembled several hours in advance, covered with plastic wrap, and refrigerated until ready to bake.

For best results, use perforated pizza pans. If you only want to bake one focaccia, wrap the second one in plastic wrap and then in aluminum foil, and freeze it for another time.

■ MAKES TWO 16-INCH FOCACCE; SERVES 16

2 large sweet red peppers (about 1 pound)
2 large sweet yellow peppers (about 1 pound)
¼ cup extra-virgin olive oil
2 medium onions, thinly sliced
2 tablespoons red wine vinegar
¼ pound thinly sliced soppressata, diced
Fine sea salt to taste
1 recipe Straight Dough (page 21)
6 tablespoons fresh rosemary needles
Coarse sea salt for sprinkling

Preheat the broiler. Lightly spray the broiler pan with olive oil spray. Place the peppers on the pan so they are not touching one another and broil, turning them often with kitchen tongs, until they are blackened all over, 8 to 10 minutes. (Alternately, grill the peppers over a gas or charcoal grill.)

Transfer the peppers to a heavy paper bag, close the top of the bag, and let the peppers cool for about 20 minutes.

When the peppers are cool enough to handle, remove the cores and peel away the skins. With paper towels, wipe away the seeds—do not rinse the peppers under running water to remove the seeds, or you will lose the flavorful juices. Cut the peppers into thin strips and place them in a bowl along with any juices.

Heat 2 tablespoons of the olive oil in a sauté pan over medium-low heat. Stir in the onions and cook, stirring occasionally, until very soft and glazed, about 5 minutes. Raise the heat to high, stir in the vinegar, and simmer until most of the liquid has evaporated. Add the onions to the bowl with the peppers. Stir in the soppressata and salt, cover, and set aside.

Preheat the oven to 425°F.

Lightly spray two 16-inch pizza pans with olive oil spray and set aside.

continued

Spreading filling on
bottom dough

Kneading rosemary into
top dough

Rolling top dough

Covering filling with
top dough

Pinching edges of
focaccia closed

Making X in center
of top dough

Punch down the dough and turn it out onto a lightly floured surface. Knead the dough for 3 to 4 minutes, until smooth and no longer sticky. Divide the dough into 4 equal pieces, and shape each piece into a ball. Set 2 balls aside and cover them with a towel or bowl.

Roll one piece of dough into a 16½-inch round. Place the dough on one of the pizza pans. Spread half the pepper mixture evenly over the dough.

Scatter half the rosemary needles over the work surface. Place the second piece of dough on top of the rosemary and knead the needles into the dough. Roll the dough out into a 16-inch round and place it over the pepper mixture. Tightly seal the edges of the focaccia by folding the edges of the bottom dough up to meet the edges of the top dough and pinching the edges together to seal them. Brush the top of the focaccia with 1 tablespoon of the olive oil and sprinkle with coarse salt. Using scissors, cut an X in the center of the top of the focaccia.

Repeat the process with the remaining dough and filling ingredients.

Bake the focaccia for 25 to 30 minutes, until the top and bottom are browned.

Cool the focaccia slightly, then use scissors or a sharp knife to cut the focaccia into wedges.

Pizza Fritta/Fried Dough

Fried dough, one of the best fast foods I know, has been in existence since ancient times. The Romans made and sold it in the local *friggitoria* (fry shop). The golden brown disks were drenched in honey and eaten on the run. As simple as this modern-day recipe appears, there are some important pointers for success. Always use fresh oil. Use a deep-fryer with a temperature gauge for even cooking and make sure the temperature of the oil is 375°F. If you don't have a thermometer, pinch off a marble-size piece of dough and test it in the oil. If it bobs to the top and browns quickly and evenly, the oil is at the proper temperature. And, finally, drain the fried dough pieces well on brown paper before tossing them in the sugar mixture. ■ MAKES 16 ROUNDS

1 recipe Straight Dough (page 21)
About 6 cups vegetable oil for deep-frying
1 cup sugar
1¹/₂ teaspoons ground cinnamon

Punch down the dough and turn it out onto a lightly floured work surface. Knead the dough for 3 to 4 minutes, until smooth and no longer sticky.

Roll the dough out under your palms into a long rope, and cut it into 16 equal pieces. Roll each piece into a 4- to 5-inch round and place the rounds on clean kitchen towels. Allow to rise for about 20 minutes, until the rounds are puffy looking.

Heat the vegetable oil in a deep-fryer or deep heavy pot until it reaches 375°F. Line a baking sheet with brown paper. Mix together the sugar and cinnamon in a heavy paper bag.

Add the rounds, a few at a time, to the hot oil and fry until they are golden brown. Scoop the rounds out of the oil with a slotted spoon and drain them well on the brown paper.

Add the warm rounds, a few at a time, to the cinnamon sugar, close the bag, and shake well to coat them on all sides. Serve warm.

Fratti di Lucca/Lucca's Fried Dough

"*Finito*," I was told by the proprietor of Buccellato Taddeucci one Monday in Lucca, Tuscany, when I tried to buy a *buccellato*. These are beautiful wheels of sweet bread that Lucca is known for, and are given to children when they make their confirmation. But consolation was not two steps away, near the church of San Michele a Foro, for it was market day and the piazza was filled with vendors selling everything from Lucca's famous olive oils to handcrafted jewelry. As I browsed here and there, the smell of fresh yeast dough being fried filled the air. I quickly made my way to a colorful little booth with a sign that read *Fratti*. There I watched a trio of bakers knead, shape, and fry donut-shaped disks of yeast dough. Then the fratti were quickly coated in sugar and sold to the throngs of people who gobbled them up like hotcakes. Eating just one of these lemon-flavored fratti is not possible; they are delicious and best when eaten hot, with the sugar sticking to your fingers and your lips.

■ MAKES 2 DOZEN FRATTI

2 tablespoons grated lemon zest
1 recipe Straight Dough (page 21)
About 6 cups vegetable oil for deep-frying
1 cup sugar

Lightly sprinkle a work surface with flour, then sprinkle the lemon zest over the work surface.

Punch down the risen dough, turn it out onto the work surface, and knead the dough, incorporating the lemon zest, for 3 to 4 minutes, until smooth and no longer sticky. Divide the dough into 2 equal pieces. Set one piece aside, covered with a towel or bowl.

Roll the dough under the palms of your hands into a 12-inch-long log. Cut the log into 12 pieces. Roll each piece under the palm of your hand into a ball and place on a clean kitchen towel. Repeat with the remaining dough, cover with another towel, and let rise for 30 minutes.

Heat the oil in a deep-fryer or deep heavy pot to 375°F. Line a baking sheet with brown paper. Place the sugar in a heavy brown bag and set aside.

Make a hole in the center of each ball with your thumb. Use your thumbs to rotate and stretch the dough out from the center hole into a 3-inch-wide donut. Fry the rounds, a few at a time, until they are golden brown on both sides. Use a slotted spoon to remove the donuts to the lined baking sheet and let drain well.

Place the warm donuts in the paper bag with the sugar. Close the top of the bag and shake vigorously to coat them evenly. Remove the donuts to a serving dish and serve immediately.

Tangy Tomato Logs

Dried tomatoes have many uses: in sauces, stews, salads, antipasto, and sandwiches. I also add them to half the Straight Dough to make a pair of rustic, crunchy bread logs that are great with cheeses such as Asiago and Taleggio. While you're at it, why not use the remaining dough to make Speckled Spinach Bread (page 52)? Or use all the dough and double the amount of dried tomatoes (and olives, if you like) to make four logs. The logs freeze beautifully.

■ MAKES TWO 16-INCH-LONG LOGS

1/2 recipe Straight Dough (page 21)
1/2 cup diced homemade (page 138) or store-bought dried tomatoes in olive oil, drained
1/4 cup diced oil-cured black olives (optional)

Lightly spray a baking sheet with olive oil spray.

Punch down the dough and turn it out onto a lightly floured surface. Knead the dough for 3 to 4 minutes, until smooth and no longer sticky. Divide the dough into 2 equal pieces. Work with one piece at a time, keeping the other piece covered with a towel or a bowl.

Roll the dough out into a 10-inch round. Spread half the tomatoes and half the olives, if desired, over the dough. Roll the dough up like a jelly roll, beginning at the side nearest you. Pinch the seam closed.

Fold the dough in half and knead it until the tomatoes and olives burst through the dough. The dough will be wet because of the tomatoes, but will come together as you knead it. If you must, add only enough additional flour to the work surface to keep the dough from sticking. With lightly floured hands, roll the dough into a 16-inch-long log. Place the log on the greased baking sheet. With scissors, make alternating 1/2-inch-deep diagonal slits 2 inches apart on either side of the log.

Repeat the process with the remaining dough, leaving a 3-inch space between the 2 logs on the baking sheet. Cover the logs with a clean cloth and let rise for 30 minutes.

Preheat the oven to 425°F.

Bake the logs for 30 to 35 minutes, until they are nicely browned on the top and underside. Remove the logs to a rack to cool completely.

Italian Country Chicken Pie

Cortona, a beautiful ancient walled city in eastern Tuscany, is perched high atop Mt. Sant'Egidio. Below the city stretches the verdant Val di Chiana with its landscape reminiscent of a Pinturicchio painting. In my short stay there, I did what all the Cortonese did, blending in with the locals on a daily basis to take the local *passeggiata* (walk about town) and do my daily shopping. On Saturdays, I headed to the Piazza del Duomo (the church square) to buy vegetables, fruit, fish, and *porchetta* sandwiches from the vendors who had set up outdoor stalls. Not to be missed was the "chicken lady," who sold spit-roasted, free-range chickens that were simply *ottimi* (the best). Returning home, I craved those chickens and found a local "chicken lady" who supplies me whenever that craving surfaces. I buy several at a time and if there are any leftovers, they go into this tasty chicken pie.

■ MAKES ONE 9-INCH PIE; SERVES 8

$3^1/2$ cups diced cooked chicken (from a $1^3/4$-pound chicken), skin removed

1 tablespoon plus 1 teaspoon extra-virgin olive oil

1 pound broccoli, cut into small florets (4 cups lightly packed)

$1/3$ cup chicken broth

2 tablespoons minced fresh flat-leaf parsley

$1/2$ cup diced roasted (see page 27 for instructions) sweet red peppers

$3/4$ teaspoon crushed juniper berries

1 teaspoon fine sea salt

$1/2$ cup diced onions

1 recipe Straight Dough (page 21)

1 egg beaten with 1 teaspoon water for egg wash

Place the chicken in a bowl and set aside.

Heat 1 tablespoon of the olive oil in a large sauté pan over medium heat. Add the broccoli florets and cook, stirring frequently, for 3 to 4 minutes, until tender. Add the chicken broth and simmer until the broth has evaporated. Stir in the parsley, roasted peppers, juniper berries, and salt and cook for 2 minutes more. Transfer the mixture to the bowl with the chicken.

In the same pan, heat the remaining 1 teaspoon olive oil over low heat. Add the onions and cook until wilted and golden brown. Add the onions to the chicken mixture and stir well to blend all the ingredients. Set aside.

Generously spray a 9- by 2-inch springform pan with olive oil spray. Set aside.

Punch down the risen dough and turn it out onto a lightly floured surface. Knead the dough for 3 to 4 minutes, until smooth and no longer sticky. Divide the dough in half. Work with one half at a time, keeping the remaining dough covered with a towel or bowl.

Roll one half of the dough out into a 14-inch round. Lightly dust the dough with flour and fold it in quarters. Place the dough in the pan, unfold it, and fit it into the pan, letting the excess dough hang over the sides. Spread the chicken filling evenly in the pan.

continued

Roll the second piece of dough out into a 14-inch round, lightly dust it with flour, and fold it in quarters. Unfold the dough over the top of the filling, letting the excess hang over the edges of the pan.

With scissors, trim the edges of the dough, leaving about a 1/2-inch overhang. Pinch the edges together, pressing them lightly down into the inside of the pan.

Gather up the dough scraps. Pinch off a lemon-size piece of dough and roll it out into a 6-inch round. Use a small canapé or cookie cutter to cut out decorative shapes to make a design on the top of the pie. Brush one side of each shape with egg wash and place egg wash side down on the top of the pie; refrigerate the remaining egg wash. (Use the remaining dough—about 12 ounces—to make a small loaf of bread, rolls, or a pizza. Or freeze it for future use.)

Cover the pie with a clean towel and let rise for 45 minutes.

Preheat the oven to 375°F.

Brush the top of the pie with the egg wash. Bake for 35 to 45 minutes, until the top of the pie is a rich brown color. Let the pie cool in the pan on a cooling rack until warm, then release the spring on the pan, and carefully remove the sides.

With a metal spatula, carefully slide the pie from the pan bottom onto a serving dish. With a sharp knife, cut the pie into wedges to serve.

Iris/Sicilian Ricotta and Chocolate Pies

As soon as I spotted *iris*, typical Sicilian street food, in the Capo market in Palermo, I knew I had to try one of these beautiful golden disks of yeast dough, coated with crunchy bread crumbs and cinnamon sugar. From the inside, a pleasant surprise of warm soft and creamy sheep's milk ricotta cheese, sweetened with sugar and mixed with chunks of chocolate, oozed out. I even found myself licking my fingers after this most satisfying culinary experience. Since sheep's milk ricotta cheese is not easy to find, use skim milk ricotta. Iris are best eaten the day they are made.

■ MAKES 1 DOZEN IRIS

FILLING

1 pound skim milk ricotta cheese, well drained

4 ounces milk chocolate, coarsely chopped

1³⁄4 cups sugar

1 teaspoon grated lemon zest

1 teaspoon grated orange zest

4 large eggs

2 cups fine dry bread crumbs

1 tablespoon ground cinnamon

1 recipe Straight Dough (page 21)

About 6 cups vegetable oil for deep-frying

In a small bowl, combine the cheese, chocolate, ¼ cup of the sugar, and the lemon and orange zests and stir to blend. Cover and refrigerate until ready to use.

Crack the eggs into another small bowl. Beat them slightly with a fork and set aside.

Pour the bread crumbs into a medium bowl and set aside.

Place the remaining 1½ cups sugar and the cinnamon in a heavy paper bag. Fold over the top, shake to blend the ingredients well, and set aside.

Punch down the risen dough and turn it out onto a lightly floured work surface. Knead the dough for 3 to 4 minutes, until smooth and no longer sticky. Roll the dough out into an 18-inch circle. Using a 3-inch round cutter, cut circles from the dough. Place the circles on clean dish towels, about 1 inch apart. Reroll the scraps and cut enough circles to make 24 in all.

Place 2 tablespoons of the filling in the center of each of 12 of the circles. Brush the edges lightly

with some of the beaten eggs. Cover with the remaining circles and seal the edges with your fingers. Then pinch the edges together all around to seal.

continued

Cutting circles with
biscuit cutter

Putting filling on
dough circles

Brushing edges of dough
with egg wash

Pinching iris edges closed

Coating iris with
bread crumbs

Carefully lift each filled round with your fingers and dip it in the beaten eggs, turning to coat on both sides. Then gently coat each round with the bread crumbs and place the rounds on cookie sheets, leaving some space between each one.

In a deep-fryer or deep heavy pan, heat the vegetable oil to 375°F. Fry the iris a few at a time until they puff up and are browned on the bottom. Turn and cook until browned on the other side. With a slotted spoon, remove the iris to brown paper to drain well.

While they are still warm, place the iris one at a time in the bag with the sugar and cinnamon and gently shake to coat them. Place the iris on a decorative platter and serve warm.

Mushrooms

One fall day, I was taking in the food scene in the arcaded markets of Reggio Emilia with my good friend Lorenza Iori. I told Lorenza that I was particularly interested in seeing some bread making, both traditional and not so traditional. She took me to Panificio Melli, where I saw and tasted all the local specialties, from *erbazzone,* a tangy beet tart, to *chizze,* small pieces of puff pastry filled with Parmigiano-Reggiano cheese and baked. But it was the window display of mushroom-shaped rolls and breads that caught my attention and I knew I had to make them, if only for their very clever resemblance to the real thing. Either the Straight Dough or the Simply Sweet Dough (page 87) can be used to make these. Pile them up in a rustic basket and use them as the centerpiece to a country supper.

■ MAKES 20 ROLLS

1 recipe Straight Dough (page 21)

Lightly spray two baking sheets with olive oil spray and set aside.

Punch down the risen dough and turn it out onto a lightly floured work surface. Knead the dough for 3 to 4 minutes, until smooth and no longer sticky. Roll the dough out under your palms to a 20-inch-long log.

With a sharp knife, cut the log into 20 pieces. Roll 10 of the pieces under the palm of your hand into 2-inch-wide slightly flattened balls. Space them 1 inch apart on a prepared baking sheet; these are your mushroom caps. Cover with a clean towel and set aside.

Roll the remaining 10 pieces into 3-inch-long "mushroom stems" and space them 1 inch apart on the second baking sheet. Cover with a towel and let the mushroom caps and stems rise for 20 minutes.

Preheat the oven to 375°F.

Bake the rolls for 20 to 25 minutes, until they just begin to color—they should remain pale, like a button mushroom. Remove the mushroom caps and stems to a rack to cool completely.

With a small sharp knife, make a slit in the underside of each mushroom cap just wide enough to accommodate a stem, ensuring a tight fit. Wedge the stems into the mushroom caps. Place them on a decorative serving dish or in a basket and wait for everyone to say, "Where did you find such beautiful mushrooms?"

Tuscan Rosemary and Currant Rolls

One fall, I rented a wonderful country house in Cortona, Tuscany, and immersed myself in the culture and life of this ancient Umbrian-Etruscan city. On market days I shopped for vegetables and fruits near the Piazza del Duomo and stood in line with all the other Cortonese waiting to buy their beloved *porchetta* (roast pork) sandwiches. Then I made my way to Via Dardano to buy the local pecorino cheese, *pesche bianche* (white peaches), and salame. In the *pasticceria,* I bought bread and biscotti. Sometimes I bought flour to make my own rosemary and currant rolls, a favorite afternoon *merenda* (snack) with Tuscan schoolchildren and adults, too.

■ MAKES 1 DOZEN ROLLS

3 tablespoons extra-virgin olive oil
2 to 3 tablespoons fresh rosemary needles, minced
1/2 cup currants or chopped dark raisins
1 recipe Straight Dough (page 21)
1 egg, slightly beaten

Heat the oil in a small skillet over low heat. Add the rosemary and cook for about 2 minutes, pressing on the rosemary with the back of a wooden spoon to release its oil. Stir in the currants or raisins and cook for 1 minute. Set aside.

Lightly spray two baking sheets with olive oil; spray and set aside.

Punch down the dough with your fists and turn it out onto a lightly floured surface. Knead for 3 to 4 minutes, until smooth and no longer sticky. Roll the dough out into a 14-inch round. Spread the rosemary mixture over the dough and brush it evenly over the surface. Roll the dough up like a jelly roll, tucking in the ends as you go. Pinch the seam closed.

Knead the dough into a ball to distribute the currants and rosemary. The dough will be wet and sticky at first, but as you knead it, it will come together. Roll the dough out under your palms to form a long rope and cut it into 12 equal pieces. On the floured surface, roll each piece into a smooth round ball.

Place the balls 1 inch apart on the prepared baking sheets. Brush the tops of the balls with the beaten egg. Cut an X in the top of each one with scissors. Cover the balls with a clean cloth and let rise for about 30 minutes, until they are puffy looking.

Preheat the oven to 375°F.

Bake the rolls for about 20 minutes, until they are browned on the top and bottom. Remove the rolls to a rack to cool completely.

Note: These freeze well if wrapped individually in aluminum foil and then placed in a Ziploc bag. Allow the rolls to defrost, unwrapped, at room temperature. Reheat in a preheated 325°F oven for about 5 minutes.

Pizza Quattro Stagioni/Four Seasons Pizza

The name of this pizza, *quattro stagioni* (four seasons), should tell you that it is as much fun to make as it is to eat. There are many versions of this compartmentalized pizza to be found in Italy, and the toppings vary widely because it is made with whatever ingredients happen to be on hand. This one evokes the seasons with everything from spring artichokes and summer tomatoes to pungent fall olives and winter onions. I like to bake this on a preheated baking stone, but conventional pizza pans are fine, too.

■ MAKES TWO 14-INCH PIZZE; SERVES 12 TO 16

TOPPINGS

5 tablespoons extra-virgin olive oil

2 large white or Spanish onions, thinly sliced

6 tablespoons red wine vinegar

4 shallots, thinly sliced

Two 14-ounce cans artichoke hearts, drained and thinly sliced

Fine sea salt and freshly ground black pepper to taste

1 recipe Straight Dough (page 21)

1/2 cup diced pitted oil-cured black olives

1/2 cup diced pitted green olives in brine

1/2 cup seeded and thinly sliced sweet red peppers

1/2 cup seeded and thinly sliced sweet yellow peppers

2 medium plum tomatoes, sliced

1/2 pound fresh mozzarella cheese, sliced

4 fresh basil leaves, shredded

In a medium skillet, heat 2 tablespoons of the oil over medium heat. Add the onions and cook, stirring often, until they are browned and glazed. Raise the heat to high, splash in the vinegar, and stir until the vinegar evaporates. Remove the onions to a small bowl and set aside.

Add 1 tablespoon of oil to the skillet and the shallots, and cook until soft. Stir in the artichoke hearts and salt and pepper and cook for 3 minutes, stirring occasionally. Remove the mixture to a small bowl.

Preheat the oven to 425°F. If using a baking stone, place it on the lowest oven rack to preheat. Alternatively, lightly spray two 14-inch pizza pans with olive oil spray and set aside. Line a baker's peel (or two peels, if you have them) with parchment paper or sprinkle heavily with cornmeal.

Punch down the dough and turn it out onto a lightly floured surface. Knead the dough for 2 to 3 minutes, until smooth and no longer sticky. Divide it in half. Set one half of the dough aside and cover with a damp towel.

Pinch off a piece of dough the size of a tangerine and set it aside. Roll the rest of the dough out to a 14-inch round.

Place the dough on the baker's peel or a baking sheet. Divide the tangerine-size piece of dough in half and with the palms of your hands, roll each piece into a 14-inch rope. Cross the two ropes over the top of the dough, dividing it into quarters.

continued

Spread half the onions over one quarter of the dough. Spread half the shallots and artichokes over the second quarter. Press half the black and green olives gently into the dough in the third quarter, and spread half of the strips of red and yellow peppers over the olives. Arrange half of the tomato slices and cheese in the last quarter and sprinkle with half the basil. Drizzle the top of the pizza with 1 tablespoon of the olive oil. Repeat the process with the remaining dough and toppings.

If using a baking stone, slide one pizza onto the stone, with the parchment paper if you used it, and bake for 15 to 20 minutes, until the top is golden brown and the bottom crust is browned and crisp. Bake the second pizza as soon as the first one is done. If using pizza pans, bake the pizzas for 25 to 30 minutes.

Cut the pizzas into wedges with scissors and serve hot.

Spicy Mustard, Potato, and Red Onion Pizza

This slightly unconventional potato-and-red-onion-topped pizza has lots of zip and tang because of the thin coating of spicy mustard over the dough. Caciocavallo cheese is a cow's milk cheese that is shaped something like a melon. It is sold in pairs, tied together with string. If it is unavailable, substitute mozzarella cheese.

■ MAKES TWO 13- TO 14-INCH PIZZE;
SERVES 12 TO 16

2 tablespoons extra-virgin olive oil, or more if necessary
2 medium red onions (1/2 pound), thinly sliced
2 teaspoons sugar
3 medium all-purpose potatoes (3/4 pound), peeled and sliced 1/4 inch thick
1 recipe Straight Dough (page 21)
1/4 cup spicy mustard, homemade (page 137) or store-bought
2 tablespoons minced fresh thyme
3/4 pound caciocavallo cheese, grated
Fine sea salt to taste

Heat 1 tablespoon of the olive oil in a large sauté pan over medium heat. Add the onions and 1 teaspoon of the sugar and cook until the onions are soft, glazed, and starting to brown, 5 to 8 minutes. Remove the onions to a bowl and set aside.

Add the remaining 1 tablespoon olive oil and 1 teaspoon sugar to the pan. Cook the potatoes, in batches if necessary, stirring often and adding additional olive oil if the pan is dry, until the potatoes just begin to brown. Remove the potatoes to a bowl and set aside.

Preheat the oven to 425°F.

Lightly spray two 13- or 14-inch pizza pans with olive oil spray and set aside.

Punch down the dough and turn it out onto a lightly floured work surface. Knead the dough for 3 to 4 minutes, until smooth and no longer sticky. Divide the dough in half. Work with one piece at a time, keeping the second piece covered with a towel or bowl.

On a lightly floured surface, roll the dough out to fit a pizza pan. Place the dough on one of the prepared pans and brush 2 tablespoons of the mustard evenly over the surface. Sprinkle 1 tablespoon of the thyme evenly over the dough.

Arrange half the potatoes over the dough. Scatter half the onions over the potatoes. Sprinkle on half the cheese and sea salt to taste.

Repeat the process with the remaining dough and topping ingredients.

Bake the pizze for 25 to 30 minutes, until the tops are golden brown, the cheese is melted, and the bottom of the crust is crisp and evenly browned. Remove the pizze to a cutting board, and cut into wedges with scissors. Serve immediately.

Variation: Scatter a combination of black and green oil-cured olives over the pizze halfway through the baking.

Nonna's Tomato Pizzette

Like every Italian cook I know, I have my favorite recipe for *pizza fritta*, or fried dough rounds. They are so easy to make, fashioned from rough pieces of the Straight Dough. Each one is a little different from the next, which is part of their charm. Usually they are deep-fried, sugared, and eaten immediately. But in this version, the *pizze fritte* are topped with tomato sauce and either smooth and creamy Fontina or delicate fresh mozzarella cheese and quickly run under the broiler to melt the cheese. They are just as delicious as their sugared cousins. ■ MAKES 12 TO 14 PIZZETTE

1 recipe Straight Dough (page 21)
About 6 cups vegetable oil for deep-frying
*2 cups tomato sauce, homemade (page 139) or
    store-bought*
*1 pound Italian Fontina or fresh mozzarella
    cheese, diced*
Fresh basil leaves for garnish

Punch down the dough and turn it out onto a lightly floured surface. Knead it for 3 to 4 minutes, until smooth and no longer sticky.

Divide the dough into 12 to 14 pieces. Shape them with your hands into rough 3- to 4-inch rounds. Place the rounds on a clean cloth and set aside.

Preheat the broiler. In a deep-fryer or deep heavy pot, heat the vegetable oil to 375°F. Fry the rounds, a few at a time, until they are golden brown. Remove them with a slotted spoon to brown paper to drain.

Place the rounds on the broiler pan and spread each one with about 2 tablespoons of the tomato sauce. Top with the cheese. Place the pan 5 inches from the heat and broil just until the cheese begins to melt. Garnish each round with a basil leaf. Serve immediately.

Fennel and Pork Calzones

A calzone is a turnover, a half-moon shape that is as popular in Italy as pizza. But unlike a pizza, which sports its toppings, a calzone tempts us with a filling inside. Calzones, like pizza, have an infinite variety of fillings. One of my favorites has always been these calzones stuffed with fennel-flavored ground pork. They make perfect eating anytime, from picnics to Sunday night supper. Ask the butcher to grind pork butt for the sausage; it is more flavorful than the often-used pork shoulder. ■ MAKES 12 CALZONES

2 pounds ground pork butt
1 large onion, minced
3 cloves garlic, minced
2 ribs celery, minced
1 carrot, minced
1 sweet yellow or red pepper, cored, seeded, and
* diced*
1 tablespoon fennel seeds
1/2 cup tomato sauce, homemade (page 139) or
* store-bought*
Fine sea salt and coarsely ground black pepper to
* taste*
1 recipe Straight Dough (page 21)
1 egg, slightly beaten
Sesame seeds for sprinkling

In a sauté pan, brown the pork in its own fat, along with the onion and garlic. Pour off the fat.

Add the celery, carrot, sweet pepper, and fennel and cook, stirring occasionally, until the vegetables are soft; the mixture is fairly dry. Transfer the mixture to a bowl and stir in the tomato sauce. Season with salt and pepper. Set the mixture aside to cool while you roll out the dough.

Punch down the dough, then turn it out onto a lightly floured surface and knead it for 3 to 4 minutes, until smooth and no longer sticky. Divide the dough into 12 equal pieces. Work with one piece at a time, keeping the remaining dough covered with a towel.

Roll each piece out on the floured surface into a 6- to 7-inch round. Spread about 1/3 cup of the filling over one half of each round. Fold the dough over the filling to form a turnover or half-moon shape, and crimp and seal the edges with a fork dipped in flour.

Place the calzones at least 1 inch apart on baking sheets that have been sprayed with olive oil spray. Brush the tops of the calzones with the beaten egg and sprinkle sesame seeds over the tops. With scissors, cut a small X in the center of each calzone. Allow the calzones to rise for 20 minutes.

Preheat the oven to 375°F.

Bake the calzones for 25 to 30 minutes, until they are golden brown on the top and bottom. Remove them from the baking sheets with a wide spatula and let them cool slightly on cooling racks. These are best eaten warm.

Scallop and Haddock Pie

Succulent sea scallops and chunks of delicate haddock blanketed in a white herb sauce make a wonderful seafood pie that is a meal in itself. To save time, you can make the Straight Dough the day before, punch it down after the first rising, and refrigerate it overnight. The next day, allow the dough to come to room temperature and rise again, then proceed with the recipe. This pie looks impressive when made in a nine-inch springform pan, so it can be unmolded, but it can also be assembled in a deep nine-inch oven-to-table casserole dish.

- MAKES ONE 9-INCH PIE; SERVES 6 TO 8

FILLING
2 tablespoons butter
1 small zucchini (about 6 ounces), diced
1 small yellow squash (about 6 ounces), diced
1 small red onion, thinly sliced
1 rib celery with leaves, thinly sliced
1/2 teaspoon celery salt
1 tablespoon salt-packed capers, rinsed and minced
3/4 pound sea scallops, patted dry with paper towels
3/4 pound haddock fillet, cut into 1-inch chunks

WHITE SAUCE
2 tablespoons butter
1/4 cup unbleached all-purpose flour
2 cups milk
2 tablespoons minced fresh flat-leaf parsley
1 tablespoon fresh thyme leaves
2 teaspoons fine sea salt
1 recipe Straight Dough (page 21)
1 egg, slightly beaten

In a large nonstick sauté pan, melt 1 tablespoon of the butter over medium heat. Add the zucchini, squash, onion, and celery and cook, stirring, just until the vegetables begin to take on a little color; they should remain al dente, somewhat firm. Sprinkle with the celery salt and the capers, blend well with a spoon, and transfer to a large bowl.

Wipe the pan clean with a paper towel. Melt the remaining 1 tablespoon butter over medium heat. Add the scallops and cook, stirring, just until they start to brown around the edges. Transfer the scallops to the bowl with the vegetables.

Add the haddock to the pan and cook just until the pieces begin to turn opaque; turn the pieces only once, or they will break apart. Transfer the haddock to the bowl with the scallops.

To make the sauce, melt the butter in a medium saucepan over medium heat. Whisk in the flour and cook, stirring, for 1 minute, until the mixture is smooth. Slowly whisk in the milk and continue whisking until the sauce comes to a simmer and thickens enough to coat the back of a spoon. Stir in the parsley, thyme, and salt.

Pour the sauce over the vegetable and seafood mixture and gently combine the ingredients with a large rubber spatula. Set aside while you roll out the dough.

Spray a 9- by 2-inch springform pan or a deep 9-inch round casserole with vegetable oil spray and set aside.

Punch down the dough and turn it out onto a lightly floured surface. Knead it for 3 to 4 minutes, until smooth and no longer sticky. Divide the dough in half. Work with one half at a time, and keep the other half covered with a towel or bowl.

Roll one piece of dough out into a 13-inch round. Line the prepared pan with the dough, without stretching it, and let the excess dough hang over the edges of the pan. Spoon the vegetable and seafood mixture into the dough-lined pan.

Roll the second piece of dough out into a 13-inch round. Place it over the top of the filling, allowing the excess to hang over the edges of the pan. With scissors, cut off the excess dough, leaving about a 1 inch overhang. Set the dough scraps aside. Pinch the edges together, pressing them gently into the inside of the pan.

Roll out the excess dough, and use a fancy cookie cutter to cut out a decorative shape, such as a starfish or fish, for the top of the pie dough. (Or use the dough to make several small round or oval rolls to bake along with the seafood pie.) Cover the pie with a clean towel and let it rise for 30 minutes.

Preheat the oven to 400°F.

Brush the top of the pie with the beaten egg. Bake for 40 to 45 minutes, until the top is golden brown and the edges of the pie have moved slightly away from the pan.

Remove the pan to a rack to cool for 15 minutes. If using a springform pan, carefully release the spring. Run a table knife around the edge of the pie and remove the sides of the pan. Place the pie on a serving platter, still on its base. Cut the pie into wedges to serve. If using a casserole dish, cut the pie into wedges with a knife and scoop out with a large serving spoon.

Speckled Spinach Bread

This wonderful round Speckled Spinach Bread is made with just half of the Straight Dough recipe. While you're at it, use the remaining dough for sharp and Tangy Tomato Logs (page 33) to add color and variety to your party table. Be sure to squeeze the spinach as dry as possible before incorporating it into the dough. You can use a 2-inch-deep baking dish or a soufflé dish, or even a charlotte mold (see Basic Equipment, page 4) to bake the bread. A 9-inch pie dish will work too, but the bread will be flatter. Serve the bread warm with a selection of cheeses such as Pecorino (a sheep's milk cheese) with black peppercorns, Parmigiano-Reggiano, creamy Fontina, and Taleggio. Add some brine-cured green and black olives for a tempting and unusual antipasto.

■ MAKES 1 ROUND LOAF

One 10-ounce package frozen chopped spinach, thawed
1 teaspoon celery salt
1/4 cup freshly grated Pecorino Romano cheese
1/2 recipe Straight Dough (page 21)

Spray a 7- by 2-inch round baking dish or a 9-inch pie dish with olive oil spray and set aside.

Cook the spinach according to the package directions. Drain the spinach in a colander and press on it well with the back of a wooden spoon to remove as much water as possible. Let cool slightly, then squeeze dry with your hands.

Place the spinach in a bowl and mix in the celery salt and cheese. Set aside to cool to room temperature.

Punch down the dough and turn it out onto a lightly floured surface. Knead the dough for 3 to 4 minutes, until smooth and no longer sticky.

Roll the dough out into a 12-inch round. Spread the spinach mixture over the dough to within 1/2 inch of the edges. Beginning at the edge nearest you, roll the dough up like a jelly roll and pinch the seam closed.

Lightly flour the work surface again. Fold the roll in half and begin kneading the dough until the spinach bursts through the dough. Have a bench knife handy to help you lift and turn the dough. The dough will be very wet because of the spinach, but add only enough flour to the work surface to help you lift and turn the dough.

Rolling the spinach into
the dough

Pinching the loaf

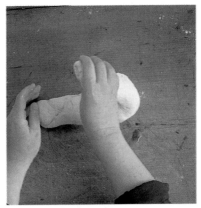

Folding the loaf

Kneading the loaf until the
spinach breaks through

Spinach breaking through the loaf

Forming the round into
the finished loaf

Continue kneading until the spinach is evenly distributed throughout the dough.

Shape the dough into a round. Use the bench
knife to lift the dough and place it in the prepared
pan. Cover the dough with a cloth and let it rise for
about 30 minutes, until almost doubled in size.

Preheat the oven to 425°F.

Bake the bread for 35 to 40 minutes, until it
sounds hollow when tapped on the bottom and the
top is golden brown. Let the bread cool in the pan
for 10 minutes.

Run a table knife around the inside edge of the
pan to loosen the bread. Carefully turn the bread
out onto a cooling rack. Turn the bread right side
up on the cooling rack. This bread is best eaten
warm. Cut into wedges or slices to serve.

Vendemmia Bread

Think of the Straight Dough as sculptor's clay. At will, you can hand-fashion shapes that will fit any occasion. One of my favorites is this easy-to-make *vendemmia* bread, so named for the grape harvest in Italy. By rolling the dough into small balls, you can make "a bunch of grapes," complete with stem and tendrils. These breads are wonderful as a fall centerpiece, to take to a wine-tasting party, or to give as a gift. To serve, just pass the "grapes" and let your guests pluck off as many as they like. For a party or a holiday like Thanksgiving, make miniature versions of these breads and set one at each place setting.

■ MAKES 2 LOAVES

1 recipe Straight Dough (page 21)
1 egg, slightly beaten
Sesame seeds for sprinkling (optional)

Lightly grease two baking sheets.

Punch down the dough and turn it out onto a floured surface. Knead it for 3 to 4 minutes, until smooth and no longer sticky. Divide the dough in half. Keep one half covered with a towel or bowl while you work with the other.

Pinch off pieces of the dough and roll them into balls: You will need twenty-two 1-inch balls and twelve 1/2-inch balls. Set two of the larger balls aside.

Form the first bunch of grapes on one of the baking sheets, keeping an inverted triangle in your mind as your guide: Start at the bottom of the bunch with one of the larger balls; use the remaining larger balls to make progressively wider rows of grapes, interspersed with a few shorter ones, as in the photograph, as you proceed to the top. To give added dimension to the bread, place the smaller balls randomly on top of the larger ones. On a floured surface, roll one of the reserved balls into a 4-inch-long stem. Attach the stem in the center of the top of the bunch of grapes, pinching to seal the seam. With scissors, cut out a V from the top of the stem. Use the remaining ball to make leaves and tendrils: Divide it in half and roll out one half on the floured surface. With a knife or decorative cutters, cut out leaves. Use the knife to make "veins"

Forming the balls of dough

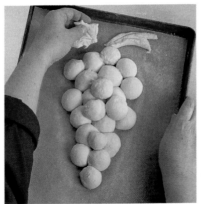

Placing the leaves and stem
on the bunch

Placing the tendrils
on the bunch

Brushing the bunch with
egg wash

Finished vendemmia ready
for rising

in the leaves, and attach to the top of the bunch of grapes. Roll the remaining dough under your palms into narrow ropes and use to make small curlicue vines that loop down the sides of the bunch.

Repeat the process with the remaining dough to make the second bunch of grapes.

Brush the grape breads with the beaten egg and sprinkle the tops with sesame seeds if you wish. Let the breads rise for only 15 minutes, or they will lose their shape as they bake.

Preheat the oven to 375°F.

Bake the breads for 30 to 35 minutes, until they are golden brown on the top and bottom. With a spatula, carefully remove the breads to a cooling rack.

This bread is best eaten warm. It can be reheated in a low oven.

Spring Spinach, Prosciutto, and Fontina Tart

In the spring, when crunchy, crisp spinach appears in my garden, I gather the leaves for this delicious tart. A bonus is that you will have enough leftover Straight Dough (about ten ounces) to make a small pizza, miniature rolls, or a handful of breadsticks. You can make and refrigerate the filling for the tart the day before assembling it. Serve the tart as a luncheon dish with a marinated carrot or tomato salad, accompanied by glasses of Pinot Grigio.

- MAKES ONE 9-INCH TART; SERVES 6 TO 8

2 pounds spinach, stemmed and washed
1 tablespoon extra-virgin olive oil
1 large clove garlic, mashed
1/4 pound prosciutto, diced
8 dried tomatoes in olive oil, homemade (page 138) or store-bought, drained and diced
1 recipe Straight Dough (page 21)
3/4 pound Italian Fontina cheese, diced
1 egg, slightly beaten
1 tablespoon sesame seeds

Place the spinach in a large saucepan, without any additional water, and cook it over medium-low heat until it wilts. Drain in a colander and squeeze out as much water as possible. Coarsely chop the spinach and put it in a small bowl.

Wipe the saucepan dry and heat the olive oil over medium heat. Add the garlic and prosciutto and cook until the prosciutto starts to brown. Add the prosciutto and garlic to the spinach. Stir in the dried tomatoes.

Lightly spray a 9- by 2-inch springform pan with olive oil spray and set aside.

Punch down the dough and turn it out onto a lightly floured surface. Knead the dough for 3 to 4 minutes, until smooth and no longer sticky. Divide the dough in half. Work with one piece at a time, keeping the remaining dough covered with a cloth or bowl.

Roll one piece of dough out on the floured surface into a 14-inch round. Line the springform pan with the dough, letting the excess dough hang over the sides of the pan. Spread half of the spinach mixture over the bottom of the dough. Spread half of the cheese over the spinach, then repeat the spinach and cheese layers.

Roll the remaining piece of dough out into an 11-inch round. With a pastry wheel, trim a 1½-inch-wide strip from two opposite sides of the round, reserving the trimmings. Then cut the remaining dough into 8 long 1-inch-wide strips. Place 4 of the strips 2 inches apart over the filling. Place the remaining strips across the first strips, at right angles, to create a lattice pattern.

With scissors, cut off the excess dough, leaving a 1-inch overhang. Turn the dough over toward the center of the tart and press it down below the rim of the pan. (Gather the dough scraps and trimmings together and reserve for another use, as suggested above.)

Brush the top of the tart with the beaten egg. Sprinkle the sesame seeds over the top and let it rise for 30 minutes.

Preheat the oven to 375°F.

Bake the tart for 30 to 35 minutes, until the crust is golden brown. Cool the tart on a rack for 30 minutes. Carefully release the spring on the pan and remove the sides of the pan. Place the tart, still on its base, on a serving dish and cut into wedges to serve.

Note: This tart can also be made in a 2-inch by 9- or 10-inch deep-dish pie pan.

Nonna's Sponge Dough

■

This is the short story of a dough made from just about nothing. It was born out of frugality, a waste-not, want-not attitude, and the ingenuity of my Nonna Galasso and my mother, both of whom could create culinary magic from just a few simple ingredients.

Although this ability applied to whatever they cooked, it was especially true for this yeast dough, which took shape from leftovers—and the definition of leftovers is generously stretched here to mean the water that was saved after potatoes were boiled for making mashed potatoes! And should even a dab of mashed potatoes be left over from the evening meal (which didn't happen very often), it too was saved with the potato water and added to the rest of the next day's dough ingredients—just little moist squares of fresh yeast, flour, and salt.

Leftover potato water can create magic in the kitchen because it contains a lot of starch, and when the water is combined with yeast, it provides a medium for yeast to grow, as it converts that starch into sugar.

I remember my mother and grandmother making this dough in the early morning. First they made the mother dough, the *madre,* or *biga,* as it is called by Italian bread bakers. The leftover potato water, yeast, and unbleached all-purpose flour were mixed together to form a loose dough that looked like thick pancake batter. This loose dough was left to ferment for several hours before they made the final dough.

As the *madre* fermented, it developed a profusion of tiny bubbles on the surface that looked very much like the holes in a kitchen sponge. In fact, this kind of starter dough is referred to as a sponge by many professional bakers. Beginning this way allowed the dough to ferment slowly, which resulted in a bread, or a pizza, or a container for vegetable pie that had a chewy, moist crumb, an airy texture, and a firm, crunchy crust.

While it baked, this dough's yeastiness permeated the entire house. When it came out of the oven, no one waited long for it to cool: The bread crackled as it was split open and a genie of perfumed steam rose from the interior to intoxicate us. We immediately reached for the olive oil or butter and made quick work of eating this moist goodness, letting the oil or butter drip down our fingers. This bread was like no other—unpretentious comfort food.

I make this dough whenever I want breads, pizza, and rolls that are dense and chewy, with that extra tang that the initial sponge provides. My favorite way to adapt the recipe is to add molasses, spices, and raisins for the Country Raisin Molasses Bread on page 72.

This dough uses less yeast than many other recipes. That allows the dough to rise more slowly and develop a more defined flavor that is in fact more in the sourdough tradition.

To make this dough, you will need to start by boiling potatoes, since the recipe calls for two cups of potato water. (Use the potatoes for Lemony Mashed Potatoes on page 132.) I make mashed potatoes for dinner the day before I want to make the dough. I refrigerate the water and the next day proceed with the recipe. Potato water will last in the refrigerator for several days, or it can be frozen for use at a later date.

Nonna's Sponge Dough

■ MAKES 2 POUNDS, 2 OUNCES DOUGH

MADRE (MOTHER DOUGH)
1/2 teaspoon active dry yeast
3/4 cup warm (110° to 115°F) potato water
1 cup unbleached all-purpose flour

SECOND DOUGH
3 1/2 to 4 cups unbleached all-purpose flour
2 teaspoons salt
1 1/4 cups warm (110° to 115°F) potato water
1 teaspoon active dry yeast
1 teaspoon olive oil

In a medium bowl, dissolve the yeast in the water and let it proof for 5 minutes; chalky-looking bubbles will appear on the surface. Stir in the flour and mix well. At this point the *madre* will be the consistency of heavy pancake batter. Cover the bowl tightly with plastic wrap and let the sponge rise for at least 3 hours or even overnight.

When the *madre* is ready, it should smell yeasty, look fluffy and light, and have a myriad of bubbles appearing on the surface. The *madre* is now ready to be combined with the additional yeast, water, flour, olive oil, and salt to make the second dough.

For detailed descriptions and illustrations of making dough by hand, either using the fontana method or in a bowl, see pages 10 and 12.

continued

Mixing the yeast and water
into the flour

Showing the pancake consistency

Fully risen sponge

Mixing sponge into
yeast mixture

Adding flour to sponge liquid

Mixing dough by hand

Mixing in olive oil

Turning out the shaggy mass

To make the second dough using a fontana, heap 3½ cups of the flour on a work surface. Add the salt and use your hands to mix the flour and salt together. Make a hole in the center of the flour with your fist.

Pour the water into the center, add the yeast, and stir with your fingers to dissolve the yeast. Let the yeast proof as above, then add the *madre* and the olive oil and mix well with your fingers. Working in a clockwise fashion, begin bringing flour from the inside of the wall into the yeast mixture with your fingers.

When a rough, shaggy mass of dough is formed, begin to knead the dough, adding additional flour as needed to make a smooth ball of dough that does not stick to your hands. Knead the dough for about 5 minutes, then cover the dough with a towel and let it rest for 5 minutes. Repeat the kneading and resting 3 more times. Each time, you will notice that the dough is easier to knead than the previous time. This is because the flour is gradually absorbing the water in the dough and allowing the gluten in the flour to relax. The dough should become soft and no longer sticky, and it should move on the work surface with ease.

Spray a large bowl with olive oil spray or coat with butter. Put the dough in the bowl, turn to coat with the oil or butter, and cover the large bowl tightly with plastic wrap. Let the dough rise for about 1½ hours, or until doubled in size.

The dough is now ready to be used in any of the recipes in this chapter. It can also be frozen, which is useful if you want to use only half the dough. Spray a heavy-duty plastic bag with vegetable oil spray, put the dough in the bag, squeeze out the air, and seal the bag. Freeze for up to 3 months.

To make the second dough in a bowl, dissolve the yeast in the water and let proof as directed above. Stir in the olive oil and the madre. Using your hands, mix in 3½ cups of the flour, about 1 cup at a time, until a shaggy dough is formed. Add the salt with the third addition of flour. Turn the dough out onto a floured work surface and begin kneading, adding additional flour as needed until a smooth ball of dough is created that is no longer sticky. Follow the directions above for kneading, resting, and rising.

To make the second dough in an electric mixer, follow the instructions on page 20, then add the olive oil to the water before you begin adding the flour. Once the dough feels soft and smooth, beat it for 5 minutes to knead, then let it rest for 5 minutes. Repeat 3 more times, then turn it out onto a floured work surface and knead by hand as described on page 13. Let rise as directed above.

Stained-Glass Tomato Tart

Make this elegant tart in the summer, when mangoes, avocados, and tomatoes are in season. The glistening fruit and vegetables look almost like stained glass on top of the tart. It is the perfect warm-weather luncheon or supper. The recipe uses only half of Nonna's Sponge Dough, but while you are at it, why not turn the remaining dough into a round loaf of bread? (See Note, page 70.)

When making this tart, be sure to use a ripe mango, but one that is not so soft that it feels soggy; an overripe mango will be difficult to cut into neat slices. Press your thumb against the mango: At the peak of ripeness, the flesh should yield to slight pressure. If it is hard, it is underripe and the taste will be bitter.

■ MAKES ONE 10½-INCH TART; SERVES 6

Juice of ½ lemon
1 medium avocado
½ recipe Nonna's Sponge Dough (page 59)
1 medium mango, peeled, seeded and thinly sliced
10 to 15 cherry tomatoes, cut in half
2 eggs, slightly beaten
¼ cup half-and-half
1 teaspoon sugar
1 tablespoon minced fresh basil
½ teaspoon fine sea salt

Spray a 10-inch tart pan with a removable bottom with olive oil spray. Place the pan on a sheet of aluminum foil and bring the edges of the foil up around but not over the sides of the pan, folding it down over itself as necessary. (This will prevent any leakage in the oven.) Set the pan aside.

Pour the lemon juice onto a plate. With a small sharp knife, peel the avocado, cut it in half lengthwise, and remove the pit. Cut the avocado into thin slices and place them on the plate with the lemon juice. Turn the slices to coat both sides with lemon juice to prevent discoloration.

Punch down the dough and turn it out onto a lightly floured surface. Knead for 3 to 4 minutes, until smooth and no longer sticky. Roll the dough out into a 12-inch circle. Place the dough in the tart pan, letting the excess dough overhang the sides, without stretching the dough: Allow enough slack so the dough will not shrink from the edges when cut.

With the rolling pin, roll over the edge of the pan to cut off excess dough. (Add the excess dough to the Sponge Dough and shape into a round to make a bonus loaf, or freeze for future use.)

Arrange the mango slices around the inside edge of the tart pan, overlapping them slightly.

continued

Wrapping the tart pan with
aluminum foil

Laying the dough into
the tart pan

Cutting the dough with a
rolling pin

Arranging the mango and
the avocado

Pouring the egg mixture
over the tart

Tart ready for oven

Make a circle of the avocado slices, partly covering the mango slices and overlapping the avocado slices slightly. Fill in the center with the tomato halves. Cover the tart with a towel and let it rise for 30 minutes.

Preheat the oven to 375°F.

In a medium bowl, whisk the eggs, half-and-half, sugar, and basil together. Sprinkle the tart with the salt and pour the egg mixture evenly over the top.

Place the tart on a baking sheet and bake for 35 to 40 minutes, until the edges of the crust are browned and the egg mixture is set. Remove the pan to a cooling rack and let cool for 45 minutes.

Remove the aluminum foil and the ring of the tart pan. With a table knife, gently loosen the tart from the bottom of the pan and slip it onto a serving dish. Cut the tart into wedges with a sharp knife. The tart is best served slightly warm or at room temperature and best eaten the day it is made.

Braided Poppy Seed Bread

This simple poppy seed bread makes wonderful sandwiches. Layer good cheese, prosciutto, or Italian salami between two slices, and you have a sandwich with structure. Or make an open-face sandwich with a slice of grilled eggplant or zucchini. What's the best summer sandwich? Mine is thinly sliced garden-fresh tomatoes sprinkled with a chiffonade of sweet basil and just a dab of mayonnaise. *Perfetto.* ■ MAKES 2 BRAIDED LOAVES

1 recipe Nonna's Sponge Dough (page 59)
1 egg, slightly beaten
1 tablespoon poppy seeds
1 teaspoon coarse sea salt

Lightly spray two baking sheets with olive oil spray.

Punch down the dough and turn it out onto a lightly floured surface. Knead the dough for 3 to 4 minutes, until smooth and no longer sticky. Divide the dough in half, then divide each half into thirds. Work with 3 pieces at a time, keeping the remaining dough covered with a towel or bowl.

Roll each piece of dough under your palms into a 14-inch-long rope. Place the 3 ropes close to each other, but not touching, on one of the baking sheets. Starting from the top, braid the 3 pieces following the photographs on page 18. Pinch the ends together and tuck underneath the braid. Repeat with the remaining dough to make the second braid.

Brush the braids with the beaten egg and sprinkle the poppy seeds and salt evenly over the tops. Cover the braids with a clean cloth and let them rise until almost doubled in size, about 25 minutes.

Preheat the oven to 400°F.

Bake the braids for about 40 minutes, until they are nicely browned on the top and bottom. Remove the braids from the oven and place on a cooling rack to cool completely. Once completely cool, the braids can be frozen. Wrap each one in aluminum foil, seal in a plastic bag, and freeze for up to 6 months. Then unwrap at room temperature and reheat in a moderate oven if desired.

Bread Basket Bread

Among the bread-making equipment in my kitchen is a banneton, a cloth-lined willow basket used for giving a nice shape to bread dough as it rises. An added bonus is that the imprint of the basket is left on the dough, creating a nice visual effect. Bannetons can be round, elongated, even oval. They are a bit expensive (see Mail-Order Sources, page 143), but you can improvise a banneton with a regular basket lined with a clean cloth. You can use a banneton to shape the dough in many of the recipes in this book, such as the Country Raisin Molasses Bread (page 72), Pane Casereccio (page 22), and Pumpkin Seed, Sage, and Pancetta Bread (page 79). ▪ MAKES 1 LOAF

Cornmeal
1 recipe Nonna's Sponge Dough (page 59)

Generously dust a 9- by 3½-inch banneton or other cloth-lined basket with flour. Sprinkle a layer of cornmeal evenly over the bottom of the basket. Set the basket aside.

Punch down the dough and turn it out onto a lightly floured surface. Knead the dough for 3 to 4 minutes, until smooth and no longer sticky. Form the dough into a round or long loaf, following the photographs on pages 17–18, and place it in the basket. Cover the basket with a clean cloth and let the dough rise for 1 to 1½ hours, until it is three quarters of the height of the basket.

Preheat the oven to 425°F.

If baking the bread on a stone, put the stone on the bottom oven rack to preheat and line a baker's peel with parchment paper. Set aside. If baking the bread on a baking sheet, spray it with olive oil or vegetable oil spray.

Remove the cloth from the top of the dough. Gently turn the basket over onto the peel or baking sheet, being careful not to deflate the dough. Make two or three shallow 2-inch-long slashes or cuts across the top of the bread with a lame, sharp knife, or scissors.

To bake the bread on the stone, slide the bread, with the parchment paper, onto the stone. Or place the baking sheet in the oven. Using a mister, mist the oven walls quickly with water and immediately close the oven door. Mist the oven walls two or three times more during the first 10 minutes of baking. Bake the bread for 30 to 35 minutes if using the baking stone, 35 to 40 minutes if baking the bread on a sheet, until the bread is a rich golden brown on the top and bottom and the bottom sounds hollow when tapped with your knuckles.

With a bread paddle or a large metal spatula, remove the bread to a rack to cool completely.

Calabrian Pitta

Pitta, a hearty filled bread that can be a meal in itself, is a Calabrian specialty. From town to town within Calabria, the "toe" of the Italian boot, the ingredients for the filling vary. My favorite is a selection of Italian cooked meats and cheeses sandwiched between two layers of colorful salad ingredients.

It's easiest to make the bread the day before you plan to fill it. The salad filling should be made in advance as well. When the pitta is cut, beautiful wedges of striped layers emerge, almost too beautiful to eat. For your next picnic, tote a pitta for a hassle-free gourmet lunch or cold supper. ■ MAKES 1 FILLED BREAD; SERVES 8

SALAD FILLING
1 cup oil-cured black olives, pitted
1 cup green olives in brine, drained and pitted
2/3 cup sliced fennel bulb

1/2 cup marinated artichoke hearts, drained
1 small sweet red pepper, cored, seeded, and cut into strips
2 cloves garlic, minced
1/2 cup chopped mixed fresh basil, flat-leaf parsley, and fennel leaves
2 tablespoons extra-virgin olive oil
Fine sea salt to taste

1 loaf Nonna's Sponge Dough bread (page 59) (see Note)

MEAT AND CHEESE FILLING
1/4 pound thinly sliced Genoa salami
1/3 pound thinly sliced prosciutto
1/3 pound thinly sliced capicolla
1/2 pound fresh or packaged mozzarella, sliced
1/2 pound thinly sliced provolone

Put the olives, fennel bulb, marinated artichokes, and pepper strips in a food processor and coarsely chop. Transfer the mixture to a bowl and add the garlic, chopped herbs, and olive oil. Blend well and season with salt. Cover the bowl and set aside to marinate for several hours.

With a bread knife, cut a 1/2-inch lid off the top of the bread and set aside. With your fingers, pull out the interior crumb of the bread, leaving about a 3/4-inch-thick shell. Reserve the inside of the bread for another use, such as Homemade Bread Crumbs, page 119.

Spread half the marinated salad ingredients evenly in the bottom of the bread shell. Layer the meats and cheeses alternately on top of the salad.

continued

Slicing the top of the loaf

Removing the crumb
from the loaf

Spooning the marinated salad
filling into the loaf

Layering the meat
and cheese

Placing the top on the
completed pitta

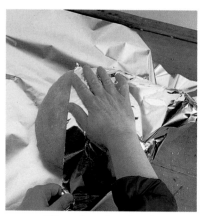

Wrapping the pitta in
aluminum foil

Spread the remaining salad over the top. Replace the bread lid. Wrap the bread tightly in aluminum foil. Place a heavy weight such as a cast-iron skillet or two clean bricks on top of the bread and refrigerate it for at least 6 hours or, even better, overnight.

An hour before serving, remove the foil and place the pitta on a serving plate. With a bread knife, cut it into wedges while it is still cold (this will ensure neatly cut wedges). Let come to room temperature before serving.

Variation: Instead of flat layers of meats and cheeses, make rolled layers by rolling slices of the cheeses and meats together into cylinders.

Note: You can either make a round loaf of Bread Basket Bread (page 67) or shape the dough into a round, as shown in the photographs on page 17, and let it rise, covered, on a parchment-lined baker's peel or a lightly oiled baking sheet (see page 22 for rising time). Then slash the dough and bake on a preheated baking stone or a baking sheet, following the procedure on page 22.

Focaccine with Herbs

Focaccia, a type of thin, crispy pizza, wears a different topping from one place to another in Italy. The more common *focacce* are sparsely covered with nothing more than a brushing of olive oil, slivers of garlic, and a dash of salt. These small versions, called *focaccine*, are rounds of dough speckled with a fine paste (*battuto*) of herbs, garlic, and olive oil. Accompanied by an assortment of cheeses, these make an ideal antipasto to be served with wine. They are equally satisfying as picnic food, and the perfect snack.

■ MAKES SIXTEEN 6-INCH ROUNDS

$1/4$ cup fresh thyme leaves
$1/4$ cups fresh tarragon leaves
$1/4$ cup fresh parsley leaves
2 tablespoons fresh basil leaves
2 large cloves garlic, peeled
3 tablespoons extra-virgin olive oil
2 teaspoons coarse sea salt
$1/2$ teaspoon coarsely ground black pepper
1 recipe Nonna's Sponge Dough (page 59)
$1/2$ cup freshly grated Parmigiano-Reggiano
   cheese

Place all the herbs and the garlic in a pile on a cutting board and finely mince them. Place the mixture in a small bowl, stir in the olive oil, salt, and pepper and mix well. Cover the bowl and let the mixture sit at room temperature for 30 minutes.

Lightly grease four large baking sheets.

Punch down the dough and turn it out onto a lightly floured surface. Knead the dough for 3 to 4 minutes, until smooth and no longer sticky. Divide the dough in half.

Roll one half of the dough into a 14-inch round. Spread half the herb mixture evenly over the surface of the dough. Sprinkle with half the cheese. Roll up tightly like a jelly roll, and pinch the seam closed.

Roll the dough under your palms into a 16-inch-long log. Cut the log into 8 pieces. Knead each piece on the floured surface until the herbs are evenly distributed throughout the dough. Roll each piece into a 6-inch round. Place the focaccine on the greased baking sheets, leaving about 2 inches between each one. Cover with a clean towel and let rise for 20 minutes. Repeat the process with the remaining dough, herb mixture, and cheese.

Preheat the oven to 400°F.

Bake the focaccine, in two batches, for 25 to 30 minutes, until they are golden brown. Cool the focaccine briefly on a cooling rack. Serve warm.

Note: These can be frozen after they're cooled completely. Wrap each one individually in aluminum foil and put in plastic bags. When ready to use, defrost, unwrapped, and heat in a preheated 325°F oven for 5 minutes.

Country Raisin Molasses Bread

Like magic, Nonna's Sponge Dough changes character with just a few choice ingredients: mahogany-colored molasses, soothing aromatic cinnamon and cloves, and plump dark raisins. *Allora*, what you have created is a dough for an impressive, chewy raisin bread that stays moist for a week! Cut thick slices of this bread for breakfast toast, or do as the ancient Romans did: Dip the slices in beaten egg and milk and cook in a skillet for wonderful Sunday morning French toast. Children will appreciate a slathering of cream cheese between two slices. I have given this bread to friends who find it so good that the entire loaf lasts but a day! It is best to make this dough in a heavy-duty stand mixer fitted with a dough hook. Do not try to make it in a food processor, as the blade cannot handle the weight of the dough. ■ MAKES 1 LARGE ROUND LOAF

1 teaspoon active dry yeast
1 1/4 cups warm (100° to 115°F) potato water
Madre for Nonna's Sponge Dough (page 59), allowed to rise
1/2 cup unsulphured dark molasses
4 1/2 to 5 cups unbleached all-purpose flour
1 teaspoon extra-virgin olive oil
1 teaspoon fine sea salt
1 teaspoon ground cinnamon
1/4 teaspoon ground cloves
1 cup dark raisins

In the bowl of a heavy-duty mixer fitted with a dough hook or batter paddle, dissolve the yeast in the potato water. Let it proof for 5 minutes, until the mixture looks chalky and small bubbles appear in clusters on the surface.

Add the *madre* to the bowl along with the molasses and blend the ingredients on low speed. Add 2 cups of the flour and blend until all the flour is incorporated. Add the olive oil, salt, cinnamon, and cloves, then add just enough additional flour to make a dough that is soft but not sticky. Blend in the raisins.

Increase the speed to high and mix the dough for 3 to 4 minutes, until it pulls away from the sides of the bowl and forms a mass of dough that does not separate. Feel the dough: If it seems too sticky, add a little more flour. It should feel like thick taffy or stiff cookie dough.

Spray a large bowl with olive oil spray and transfer the dough to the bowl, turning it several times to coat it in the olive oil. Cover the bowl tightly with plastic wrap and let it rise at room temperature (about 77°F) for 3 hours, until doubled in size.

Line a baker's peel with parchment paper or spray a baking sheet with vegetable oil spray.

Punch down the risen dough and turn it out onto a lightly floured surface. Knead it for about 4 minutes. The dough should feel soft and be uniformly smooth and no longer sticky. Fashion the dough into a round (see photographs, page 17). Place the dough on the baker's peel or baking sheet. Cover the dough with a clean towel and let it rise for 45 minutes, until almost doubled in size.

If using a baking stone to bake the bread, preheat the oven to 425°F and put the stone on the lowest oven rack to preheat. If using a baking sheet, preheat the oven to 400°F.

Make three shallow 2-inch-long slashes across the top of the bread with a lame, small sharp knife, or razor blade.

Slide the dough, with the paper, onto the baking stone, or place the baking sheet in the oven. Bake for 35 to 40 minutes if baking on a stone, 45 to 50 minutes if using a baking sheet, until the top and bottom of the bread are nicely browned and the bottom sounds hollow when tapped with your knuckles. Remove the bread to a cooling rack to cool completely.

Note: This bread will freeze beautifully for up to 3 months if wrapped in aluminum foil and then sealed in a plastic bag.

Caponata Tartlets

These delicious little caponata tartlets, with their sweet-and-sour taste, make an elegant lunch with a salad. Or tote them to a picnic or tailgate party, or make them miniature-size to serve as antipasti for a crowd. Make the caponata for the filling or use a good prepared caponata.

■ MAKES 8 TARTLETS

1 recipe Nonna's Sponge Dough (page 59)
2 cups caponata, homemade (page 140) or
   store-bought
1 egg, slightly beaten

Lightly spray eight 3½-inch fluted tartlet shells with olive oil spray and set aside.

Punch down the dough and turn it out onto a very lightly floured surface. Knead it for 3 to 4 minutes, until smooth and no longer sticky. Divide the dough into quarters.

Roll each quarter into a 12-inch round. Using a 4-inch plain biscuit cutter, cut 4 circles from each quarter. Line each tartlet shell with a dough circle, stretching it to allow the excess dough to hang over the edges of the shell.

Place 2 heaping tablespoons of the caponata in each tartlet pan, spreading it evenly to the edges.

Place one of the remaining dough circles on top of each tartlet and pinch the edges of the dough together to seal. Cover the tartlets with a towel and let rise for 20 minutes.

Preheat the oven to 375°F.

With scissors, cut an X in the center of each tartlet. Brush the tops of the tartlets with the beaten egg. Place the tartlets on two baking sheets and bake for 25 minutes, until the tops are golden brown.

Remove the tartlets to a cooling rack to cool for 10 minutes. With the tip of a table knife, carefully lift each tartlet out of its shell and allow to cool on the rack. Serve slightly warm or at room temperature.

Cutting the flattened dough
with biscuit cutter

Placing the dough in the
tartlet mold

Filling the tartlet with caponata

Placing the cover on
the tartlet

Pinching the cover

Cutting an X with scissors

Brushing the dough with
egg wash

Finished tartlet ready
for baking

Grilled Pizza

Triumph was mine the day I made grilled pizza from Nonna's Sponge Dough. It worked like a charm on my gas grill, but it is even better if you can use hardwood charcoal to impart that subtle smoky flavor to this wonderfully light dough. The dough cooks to a perfectly crisp crust, with those "designer" grill marks on the bottom besides. The topping for this pizza is a happy marriage of dried-tomato paste, cured black olives, fresh, creamy mozzarella cheese, and fresh parsley. This recipe makes two pizzas, so you will need two baking peels or two rimless cookie sheets to transfer the pizzas to the grill.

■ MAKES TWO 12- TO 14-INCH PIZZE; SERVES 12 TO 16

1 recipe Nonna's Sponge Dough (page 59)
Cornmeal for sprinkling
20 dried tomatoes in olive oil, homemade (page 138) or store-bought, drained
1 cup pitted oil-cured black olives, cut in half
1/2 pound (2 balls) fresh mozzarella, sliced
2 tablespoons minced fresh flat-leaf parsley

Punch down the dough and turn it out onto a floured surface. Knead it for 3 to 4 minutes, until smooth and no longer sticky. Divide the dough in half. Keep one half covered with a towel or bowl while you work with the other half.

Roll the dough out into a 12- to 14-inch round, or just large enough to fit on a wooden peel or a rimless cookie sheet. Sprinkle cornmeal very liberally over the wooden peel or cookie sheet, place the dough on the cornmeal, and set aside. Repeat the process with the second half of dough.

Puree the dried tomatoes in a food processor until a paste is formed. Spread the tomato paste evenly over each round of dough. Scatter the olives, cheese, and parsley over the tomato paste.

Cover the pizzas with clean cloths and let them rise for 20 minutes.

Preheat a gas grill to 500°F or prepare a hot fire in a charcoal grill.

Slide one of the pizzas from the peel or cookie sheet onto the grill rack. If your grill has a large enough cooking surface, cook both pizzas at the same time; otherwise, cook one at a time. Cover with the lid and cook for about 10 minutes, until the underside of the crust is crisp and the grill lines are clearly defined.

Slide the peel or the cookie sheet underneath the pizza(s) and remove from the grill. Cut each pizza into wedges with kitchen scissors or a sharp knife and serve.

Pumpkin Seed, Sage, and Pancetta Bread

Inspiration for this bread comes from the many breads I have joyfully eaten all over Italy. From craggy-looking loaves of crusty Pugliese olive bread to the airy bread of Ferrara called *manina* (little hand), Italian breads have always held a fascination for me. This bread is studded with toasted pumpkin seeds and cracklings of crispy Italian bacon (*pancetta*), and perfumed with specks of fresh sage. Almost a meal by itself, it complements a bowl of homemade tomato soup perfectly. It is *the* bread to serve on your Thanksgiving table, and it is unmatched in its versatility as a sandwich bread for egg salad, grilled vegetables, cold chicken, or roast beef. ■ MAKES 1 LARGE LOAF

1 cup hulled pumpkin seeds
¹/₄ pound pancetta or unsmoked bacon, diced
   (about 1 cup)
1 recipe Nonna's Sponge Dough (page 59)
¹/₃ cup minced fresh sage

Preheat the oven to 350°F.

Spread the pumpkin seeds on a baking sheet and toast in the oven for about 7 minutes, until they just start to brown; watch carefully so they do not burn. Remove the seeds to a bowl and let them cool.

In a small skillet, sauté the pancetta or bacon over medium heat until nicely browned and crisp. Transfer to a cutting board and let it cool slightly. Mince the pancetta or bacon very fine and transfer it to a small dish.

Line a baker's peel with parchment paper or lightly grease a baking sheet.

Punch down the dough and turn it out onto a lightly floured surface. Knead it for 3 to 4 minutes, until smooth and no longer sticky. Roll the dough out into a 14-inch circle.

Sprinkle the pumpkin seeds, pancetta, and sage over the dough. Starting at the side nearest you, roll the dough up tightly and pinch the seam closed. Fold the dough in half and knead it until the filling bursts through the dough. Continue kneading until the filling ingredients are evenly dispersed throughout the dough (if some ingredients pop out, knead them back into the dough) and the dough feels smooth. Form the dough into a round loaf, following the photographs on page 17, and place it on the baker's peel or greased baking sheet. Cover the dough with a clean towel and set aside to rise for about 35 minutes, until nearly doubled in size.

If using a baking stone, preheat the oven to 425°F and put the stone on the lowest oven rack to preheat. If using a baking sheet, preheat the oven to 400°F.

Make three short shallow slashes across the top of the dough with a lame, sharp knife, or razor blade. If using a baking stone, slide the bread, with the paper, onto the stone. Or put the baking sheet in the oven. Mist the oven walls with water, then mist again once or twice during the first 10 minutes of baking. Bake the bread for 35 to 40 minutes if using a stone, 40 to 45 minutes if using a baking sheet, until it is golden brown and crusty on the top and bottom and the bottom sounds hollow when tapped. Remove the bread to a cooling rack.

Mushroom Pizza

One early September day while traveling through eastern Tuscany, I ventured off the main road and found myself in the small town of Piazza del Pero. The town was abuzz and no wonder, for a brightly colored banner strung across the entrance to the main piazza announced the Festa del Fungo (the mushroom festival). Tuscans take mushroom gathering and cooking seriously, and it is not uncommon to see people standing on street corners with baskets of deep brown porcini, brilliant orange *ovoli*, and other types of mushrooms, just waiting for a passerby to stop and strike a deal for the basket. And so I succumbed, buying a basket of still-warm-from-the-earth porcini mushrooms for thirty-five thousand lire (about twenty dollars), truly a bargain.

As soon as I returned to the old house I was renting, they went immediately to the grill with a simple coating of olive oil. They were almost too delicious to describe. To be able to buy fresh porcini at home is a rare and costly occurrence, so I make do with portobellos, those cultivated firm, meaty mushrooms with an Italian name (but aren't Italian) and the big brother to the brown cremini mushroom.

■ MAKES TWO 16-INCH PIZZE; SERVES 16

1/4 cup plus 1 teaspoon extra-virgin olive oil
1 pound red onions (about 3 large)
1 teaspoon coarsely ground black pepper
1 pound portobello mushrooms, stems removed, caps wiped clean, and sliced
1/3 cup dry red wine
1 recipe Nonna's Sponge Dough (page 59)
1 1/3 cups freshly grated Asiago or Parmigiano-Reggiano cheese (6 ounces)

Heat 2 tablespoons of the olive oil in a sauté pan over medium heat. Add the onions and cook, stirring occasionally, until they are browned and glazed. Stir in the pepper. Remove the onions to a bowl.

In the same pan, heat the remaining 2 tablespoons plus 1 teaspoon olive oil over medium heat. Add the mushrooms and cook, stirring occasionally, until the mushrooms have softened. Raise the heat to high, add the wine, and cook, stirring, until all the liquid has evaporated. Remove the mushrooms to a dish and set aside.

Preheat the oven to 425°F. If using a baking stone for baking the pizzas, preheat it for at least 30 minutes (if you have two stones, put one on the bottom oven rack and one on the middle rack to preheat). Line two wooden peels with parchment paper. If not using a stone, lightly spray two pizza pans with olive oil spray.

Punch down the dough and turn it out onto a lightly floured surface. Knead the dough for 3 to 4 minutes, until smooth and no longer sticky. Divide the dough in half.

Roll each piece of dough into a 16-inch round. Place the dough on the parchment-lined peels or on the pizza pans. Spread the onions, mushrooms, and cheese evenly over the pizzas.

If using a baking stone, slide one pizza, with the paper, onto the hot stone. (If you have two stones, bake both pizzas at the same time; if not, keep the second pizza loosely covered with a towel until ready to bake.) Or put the pizza pans into the oven.

Bake the pizza(s) for 20 to 25 minutes if using a stove, 30 to 35 minutes if using pizza pans, until the crust is nicely browned on the underside.

Remove the pizzas from the oven. If using a baking stone, shove the peel underneath the pizza and remove it from the stone. Cut into wedges with scissors and serve immediately.

Swiss Chard Pizza

Spread a covering of Swiss chard over Nonna's Sponge Dough, and speckle it with bits of pungent Gaeta or Niçoise olives and dried tomatoes—and you have created an airy, crisp pizza that will quickly become a favorite.

■ MAKES TWO 16-INCH PIZZE; SERVES 16

2½ pounds Swiss chard, stems removed and leaves washed well
Fine sea salt
¼ cup oil from the dried tomatoes
Coarsely ground black pepper to taste
1 recipe Nonna's Sponge Dough (page 59)
1 cup chopped homemade (page 138) or store-bought dried tomatoes in olive oil
⅔ cup chopped pitted Gaeta or Niçoise olives
1 cup shredded aged provolone cheese (about ¼ pound)

Bring a large pot of water to a boil. Add the Swiss chard and 1 teaspoon salt and cook, uncovered, for 5 minutes. Drain the Swiss chard in a colander. Let it cool, then squeeze as much water as possible out of the chard and coarsely chop it.

In a skillet, heat 2 tablespoons of the dried tomato oil over medium heat. Add the Swiss chard and cook, stirring, for 2 to 3 minutes, until well coated with the oil. Season with salt and pepper, remove to a bowl, and let cool.

Lightly spray two 16-inch pizza pans with olive oil spray.

Punch down the dough and turn it out onto a floured surface. Knead the dough for 3 to 4 minutes, until smooth and no longer sticky. Divide the dough in half.

Roll each piece of dough into a 17-inch round. Place the dough on the pizza pans, letting the excess dough overhang the rim, then turn in the overhanging dough to create an edge. Brush each round of dough with 1 tablespoon of the sun-dried olive oil. Spread the Swiss chard evenly over the surface of each round. Sprinkle the dried tomatoes, olives, and cheese evenly over the chard. Cover each pizza with a cloth and let rise for 20 minutes.

Preheat the oven to 375°F.

Bake the pizzas for 35 to 40 minutes, until the bottom crust is nicely browned. Serve hot, cut into wedges.

Roasted Vegetable Calzones

Travel through the region of Puglia at the heel of Italy's boot and you will eventually meet up with *calzoni*, those small pockets of dough with their fillings of cheese, the local *salame*, and/or vegetables, according to the whim of the cook. Among the most delicious are *calzoni di magro* (literally, "meager" calzones), so called because only vegetables are used in the filling. Roasting the vegetables adds depth of flavor. Mashed roasted garlic, a few herbs, and just a dab of tomato sauce are all the seasoning they need. The first bite conjures up magnificent memories of Puglia.

Prepare these in stages if you like. Make the dough, punch it down after the first rise, cover the bowl tightly, and refrigerate overnight. Bring the dough to room temperature the next day and allow to rise again before proceeding with the recipe. ■ MAKES 12 CALZONES

FILLING

1 small yellow squash
1 small zucchini
1 medium fennel bulb, trimmed
1 medium Spanish onion, peeled
1 medium sweet yellow pepper, cored, seeded, and cut into 2-inch squares
3 large cloves garlic, unpeeled
1 cup diced mozzarella cheese (about 5 ounces)
¼ cup prepared tomato sauce
¼ cup packed minced fresh flat-leaf parsley
1½ teaspoons dried oregano
Fine sea salt to taste
A grinding of black pepper

1 recipe Nonna's Sponge Dough (page 59)
1 egg, slightly beaten
Coarse sea salt for sprinkling

Preheat the oven to 425°F. Spray a 17- by 11½-inch baking pan with olive oil spray and set aside.

Cut the yellow squash, zucchini, fennel, and onion lengthwise into quarters. Cut the quarters into 2-inch chunks. Spread them in a single layer on the baking pan. Add the yellow pepper and garlic cloves to the pan.

Spray the vegetables lightly with olive oil spray and place the pan on the middle rack of the oven. Roast the vegetables for 45 minutes, until browned, turning them once, halfway through the cooking time. Remove the vegetables from the oven.

With your fingers, slip the skins from the garlic cloves and discard them. In a large bowl, mash the garlic with a fork. Add the remaining roasted vegetables, the cheese, tomato sauce, parsley, oregano, salt, and pepper. Gently toss all the ingredients with a spoon to mix well. Set aside.

Lightly coat two baking sheets with olive oil spray and set them aside.

Punch down the dough and turn it out onto a floured surface. Knead it for 3 to 4 minutes, until smooth and no longer sticky. Divide the dough in half.

Work with half the dough at a time, keeping the remaining dough covered with a cloth or bowl. Roll the dough into a 12-inch-long log. Cut the log into six pieces. On the floured surface, roll each piece of dough into a 6-inch circle. Spread a generous ¼ cup of the vegetable filling on one half of each piece of dough, leaving a ½-inch border. Fold the dough over to form a turnover. Pinch the edges closed with your fingers, then use a fork dipped in flour to crimp and seal the edges.

Space the calzones about 1 inch apart on the baking sheets. Cover them with towels and let rise for 30 minutes.

Preheat the oven to 425°F.

Cut an X in the center of each calzone with scissors. Brush the tops with the beaten egg and sprinkle each one with a little coarse sea salt.

Bake for 30 to 35 minutes, until the calzones are golden brown on top and the bottom crust is firm. Transfer the calzones to cooling racks to cool slightly. These are best eaten warm.

Calzones can be frozen for up to 2 months. Wrap individually in aluminum foil and put into plastic bags. Thaw, unwrapped, at room temperature and reheat in a preheated 325°F oven for about 5 minutes.

Note: If you have perforated pizza pans, use them instead of baking sheets. They will help to ensure even browning on the underside of the calzones and prevent a soggy bottom crust.

Simply Sweet Dough

■

Imagine yourself standing in front of a pastry shop window admiring glistening fruit tarts, moist donuts, crunchy coffee cakes, miniature teatime brioches, and plump kuchens. You do not know where to look first or, more important, what to buy first! That is how I feel whenever I make Simply Sweet Dough, which, in the pastry window of my mind, leaves me with the happy dilemma of endless possibilities.

The richness of the dough comes from eggs, butter, sugar, and milk. It is a wonderful dough to work with and yields to all kinds of coaxing and shaping. Keeping in mind a few pointers will make this a fail-proof dough every time. The key to success depends on the right ingredients. First, use filtered or bottled noncarbonated water, not regular tap water, which can affect the taste of the dough and leave a dull, insipid aftertaste. Second, make sure that the eggs and unsalted butter are wonderfully fresh. It is important that the butter and eggs be at room temperature before they are added to the yeast mixture. Third, use unbleached all-purpose hard wheat flour (see Basic Ingredients, page 1). Fourth, measure the flour correctly, using either the sprinkle and sweep method (see page 9) or a scale. Fifth, use 1 percent low-fat milk, which will inhibit the action of the yeast much less than full-fat milk.

Because butter, eggs, and milk are used in this dough, the dough is heavier than the other two master doughs in this book, which are basically just water, yeast, and flour. This dough will also rise much more slowly than the others because fats such as butter and those in milk tend to slow down the fermentation process.

When making this dough, strive to achieve a soft, stretchable dough that when kneaded will move with ease off the palms of your hands. Make the dough by hand, using a fontana or mixing in a bowl, or make it in a heavy-duty mixer fitted with a dough hook or batter paddle. For detailed descriptions and illustrations of both these hand methods, see pages 10–12. Whatever method you choose to make the dough, remember to add small amounts of flour gradually until the desired consistency is obtained. This step takes practice, but eventually you will know by feel when a sufficient amount of flour has been added.

The dough can be made the day before you want to use it. Simply let it rise once, gently deflate it in the bowl, cover the bowl tightly with plastic wrap, and refrigerate it. The next day, allow the dough to come to room temperature and rise again, until doubled in size, then proceed with the recipe.

Simply Sweet Dough

■ MAKES 2½ POUNDS DOUGH

1 package active dry yeast (0.25 ounce)
¼ cup warm (110° to 115°F) filtered or bottled
   noncarbonated water
½ cup warm (110° to 115°F) 1% low-fat milk

3 large eggs, at room temperature
4½ to 5 cups unbleached all-purpose flour
½ cup sugar
1½ teaspoons salt
8 tablespoons (1 stick) unsalted butter, softened

In a medium bowl, sprinkle the yeast over the water and mix with a spoon until the yeast dissolves. Let the mixture proof for about 5 minutes. Small clusters of chalky-looking bubbles should appear on the surface. Stir in the milk. With a fork, beat in the eggs one at a time. Set the mixture aside.

To make the dough using the fontana method, mound 4½ cups of the flour on a work surface. Add the sugar and salt, and mix well with your hands. With your fingers, break up the butter into small pieces, scattering them over the dry ingredients. Using your hands, work the ingredients together into a crumbly mixture. Make the fontana by burrowing your fist down into the middle of the flour mixture to make a hole.

Slowly pour the yeast mixture into the center of the fontana. With your fingers, begin mixing the flour from the inside wall of the fontana into the yeast mixture, working in a clockwise fashion. Continue mixing until the flour mixture thickens and a shaggy mass of dough forms. Knead the dough for 3 to 4 minutes, adding just enough of the remaining flour to create a soft but stable ball that holds its shape. Push any excess flour aside.

Let the dough rest on the work surface for 10 minutes, covered with a towel or bowl. Then knead it again for about 5 minutes, until it forms a smooth ball and is no longer sticky.

Lightly spray a large bowl with cooking oil spray or coat lightly with butter. Gather up the dough, place it in the bowl, and turn to coat. Tightly cover the bowl with plastic wrap and let the dough rise until doubled in size, 2 to 2½ hours.

To make the dough in a bowl, mix together 4½ cups of the flour, the sugar, and salt. Break up the butter over the dry ingredients and work it in with your hands until a crumbly mixture is obtained. Add the yeast mixture and mix with your hands until a ball of dough is formed. Add additional flour if necessary to obtain a dough that is soft but not too sticky.

Turn the dough out onto a floured work surface and knead it for 3 to 4 minutes, until a smooth ball of dough forms. Let the dough rest on the work surface for 10 minutes, covered with a towel or inverted bowl. Knead the dough again for 5 minutes, until smooth and no longer sticky.

Lightly spray a large bowl with cooking oil spray or lightly coat with butter. Gather up the dough, place it in the bowl, and turn to coat. Cover the bowl tightly with plastic wrap and let the dough rise until doubled in size, 2 to 2½ hours.

To make the dough in a heavy-duty mixer fitted with a dough hook or batter paddle, combine 4½ cups of the flour, the sugar, and salt in the mixer bowl. Blend on low speed to combine. Add

Crumbling/mixing butter
into dry ingredients

Texture of crumbly mixture

Adding liquids to crumbly mixture

Mixing the wet and dry
ingredients

Turning out the
shaggy mass

Dough ready to be kneaded

the butter and blend on medium speed until the mixture resembles coarse crumbs. Slowly add the yeast mixture and beat until a ball of dough is formed. Let the dough rest in the mixer for 5 minutes, then beat it again for about 3 minutes, adding additional flour only if the dough is runny or soupy. The dough is ready to be removed from the mixer when it holds its shape if you pinch it together. Turn the dough out onto a floured work surface and knead for 3 to 4 minutes, until smooth and soft. Cover the dough with a bowl and let it rest for 10 minutes. Then knead the dough again for 3 to 4 minutes, until no longer sticky, and shape it into a ball.

Lightly spray a large bowl with cooking oil spray or lightly coat with butter. Place the dough in the bowl and turn to coat. Cover the bowl with plastic wrap, and let the dough rise until doubled in size, 2 to 2½ hours.

When the dough has risen to approximately two times its size, use two fingers to make two indentations into the center of it. If the indentations do not close up, the dough is sufficiently risen and ready to use in any of the recipes in this chapter.

To freeze the dough for future use, place it in a Ziploc bag that has been sprayed with cooking oil spray. Seal the bag and freeze for up to 3 months. To use, remove the dough from the bag and place it in a bowl that has been lightly sprayed with cooking spray. Cover the bowl with plastic wrap and let the dough thaw and then rise until it is doubled in size before using.

Almost Apple Charlotte

For this recipe I have borrowed on the idea of the classic molded apple charlotte, which uses trimmed slices of bread, pureed apples, rum, and plenty of butter. But in this version, crunchy slices of apples line the bottom of the mold, nestled in a bed of cinnamon-and-clove-flavored sugar. Instead of lining the sides of the mold with strips of buttered bread, I cover the apple slices with the Simply Sweet Dough and allow it to rise before baking. Use a seven- by four-inch charlotte mold (see Basic Equipment, page 4) or another similar-sized mold, or a deep baking dish, such as a seven-inch soufflé dish. This uses only half of the sweet dough recipe, but while you are at it, why not use the remaining dough to make the Baker's Dozen Mini Brioche on page 93?

■ SERVES 6 TO 8

2 medium Granny Smith apples, peeled, cored, and thinly sliced
1 tablespoon fresh lemon juice
1/4 cup sugar
1/4 teaspoon ground cinnamon
1/4 teaspoon ground cloves
1/2 recipe Simply Sweet Dough (page 87)
Sweetened whipped cream for serving (optional)

Brush a charlotte mold or other 7- by 4-inch-deep pan with butter. Cut a piece of parchment paper to fit the bottom of the mold and brush it with butter. Set the mold aside.

In a bowl, toss the apple slices with the lemon juice. Set aside.

In a small bowl, mix the sugar, cinnamon, and cloves together. Sprinkle the sugar mixture evenly over the bottom of the prepared mold.

Drain the apple slices. Arrange 4 or 5 slices side by side in the center of the mold. Then arrange a circle of apple slices around the outer part of the mold, overlapping them slightly and partially covering the slices in the center. Line the side of the mold with a ring of apple slices, standing them curved side up; you may not need all the apple slices. Set aside.

Punch down the dough and turn it out onto a lightly floured surface. Knead the dough for 3 to 4 minutes, until smooth and no longer sticky. Shape the dough into a flattened ball just large enough to cover the apples in the bottom of the mold. Do not worry if the dough does not quite touch the apples around the sides of the mold; as it rises, it will. Cover the mold with a clean cloth and let rise for 40 minutes, until the dough has risen three quarters of the way up the mold.

continued

Sprinkling sugar mix in
charlotte mold

Overlapping apple slices in
bottom of mold

Apples lining bottom and
sides of mold

Placing dough over apples

Preheat the oven to 375°F.

Bake the charlotte for 35 to 40 minutes, until the top is golden brown and a cake skewer inserted in the center comes out clean. Cool the charlotte in the mold on a rack for 30 minutes.

Carefully run a table knife around the inside edges of the mold. Invert the charlotte onto a serving plate. Remove and discard the parchment paper. Serve the charlotte warm, cut into wedges, with a dollup of sweetened whipped cream if you wish.

Note: If the charlotte has baked so that there is a high dome on top, slice off some of the top crust with a bread knife before unmolding it so it will rest evenly on the serving dish.

Baker's Dozen Mini Brioche

Mini brioche are perfect for a brunch. You can use half the sweet dough to make the Baker's Dozen of the brioche and use the other half for the Almost Apple Charlotte on page 91 (or freeze the remaining dough for another time). Or double this recipe to make twenty-six brioche. You will need three by one-and-a-quarter-inch fluted stainless steel or disposable (but reusable of course) aluminum foil brioche molds.

■ MAKES 13 MINI BRIOCHE

1/2 recipe Simply Sweet Dough (page 87)
1 large egg
1 tablespoon milk

Coat thirteen 3- by 1¼-inch mini brioche molds or aluminum foil molds with vegetable oil spray. Place them on a baking sheet and set aside.

Punch down the dough and turn it out onto a lightly floured work surface. Knead the dough for 3 to 4 minutes, until smooth and no longer sticky.

Roll the dough under the palms of your hands into a 14-inch-long rope. Cut it into fourteen 1-inch pieces. Set one piece aside. Roll the remaining pieces into balls and place them in the prepared molds. Divide the remaining piece of dough into 13 small pieces and roll each one into a tiny round. With your thumb, make a deep indentation in the center of each brioche and place one of the tiny rounds in the center of each one. (Or cut an X in the center of each one with scissors and insert one of the tiny rounds.) Cover the molds with a clean cloth and let rise for 30 minutes.

Preheat the oven to 375°F. In a small bowl, beat the egg and milk together with a fork. Brush the top of each brioche with the egg mixture.

Bake the brioche, on the baking sheet, for 15 to 20 minutes, until they are nicely browned and shiny. Remove the molds to a rack to cool for 10 minutes. Carefully remove the brioche from the molds and let them cool completely.

Note: These are wonderful served warm with jam or butter or with lemon curd. They can be frozen if individually well wrapped in aluminum foil and placed in a plastic container.

Ciambella/Twisted Bread Ring with Prunes and Marsala

The windows of *pasticcerie* throughout Italy are filled with delirious displays of delicious-looking sweet things, but the real test is in the taste. My favorite *pasticcerìa* is still Sandri's on the main Corso Vanucci in Perugia. When I ask about particular ingredients for some of their pastries, I am always proudly told, "Tutto fatto con burro" (everything is made with butter). Some of my favorites are the dried prune pastries. In this version, inspired by Sandri's, a prune paste made with sweet Marsala wine fills the elegant-looking twisted bread ring known as *ciambella*.

■ MAKES 1 WREATH-SHAPED BREAD

FILLING

2 cups pitted dried prunes (12 ounces)
3 tablespoons sweet Marsala wine
1 tablespoon grated orange zest

1 recipe Simply Sweet Dough (page 87)
1 egg, beaten with 1 tablespoon water for egg wash
2 tablespoons turbinado (coarse brown) sugar

Put the prunes and Marsala wine in a food processor or blender and pulse to a smooth paste. Transfer the mixture to a medium bowl. Stir in the orange zest and set the mixture aside.

Lightly butter a baking sheet.

Punch down the dough and turn it out onto a floured surface. Knead the dough for 3 to 4 minutes, until smooth and no longer sticky. Roll the dough out into an 18-inch round.

With a rubber spatula, spread the prune filling evenly over the dough to within 1/2 inch of the edges. Starting at the side nearest you, roll the dough up tightly like a jelly roll, tucking in the ends as you roll. Pinch the seam closed and turn the roll seam side down.

Place the dough on the buttered baking sheet. Bring the two ends together to form a ring shape and pinch the ends firmly together so they will not

come apart as the ciambella bakes. Cover with a clean towel and let it rise for 1 1/2 hours, until doubled in size.

Preheat the oven to 375°F.

Lightly butter the outside of a small metal or heatproof glass bowl, or spray with vegetable oil spray, and place it upside down in the center hole of the ring. Or use a piece of greased aluminum foil crumpled into a ball. (This will keep the hole from closing during baking.) Brush the ring with the egg wash and sprinkle the brown sugar evenly over the top. With scissors, make 1 1/2-inch-deep slits all around the outside edge of the ring, 1 1/2 to 2 inches apart. With your hand, spread the pieces slightly apart and twist each piece to expose the cut sides.

Bake the ring on the middle rack of the oven for 30 to 35 minutes, until nicely browned on the

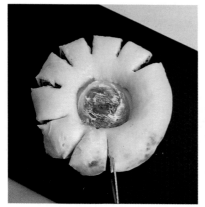  

Making decorative slits in
the ciambella

Opening ciambella slices

Slices twisted back on
themselves

top and bottom. Let the ring cool slightly on the baking sheet for 5 minutes. Carefully remove the ramekin or foil, then, with a metal spatula, transfer the ring to a rack to cool slightly.

This is best served warm. Once cooled, it can be frozen, well wrapped in foil and then in a plastic bag, for up to 2 months. Thaw, unwrapped, and serve at room temperature.

Fig, Chocolate, and Walnut Braid

This free-form lattice bread has a winning taste combination of ingredients—dried baby figs, rich chocolate, and walnuts, and it looks as elegant as it tastes. Use half the Simply Sweet Dough recipe and reserve the remaining half to make the Sweet Spiral Wreath on page 113, or another recipe.

■ MAKES ONE 14-INCH-LONG BRAID

1¹/4 cups dried whole figlets (8 ounces), stemmed and halved lengthwise
2 tablespoons orange liqueur or brandy
¹/2 recipe Simply Sweet Dough (page 87)
1 tablespoon milk
3 ounces bittersweet chocolate, coarsely chopped
¹/2 cup coarsely chopped walnuts

GLAZE
1 cup confectioners' sugar
¹/2 teaspoon vanilla extract
1¹/2 to 2 tablespoons milk or half-and-half

Place the figlets in a shallow bowl. Add the liqueur or brandy and mix well. Set aside until soft.

Lightly coat a 16- by 14-inch rimless cookie sheet with vegetable oil spray, and set aside.

Punch down the dough and turn it out onto a floured surface. Knead the dough for 3 to 4 minutes, until smooth and no longer sticky. Roll the dough out into a 14-inch square and place it on the cookie sheet.

Brush the dough with the milk. Spread the figlets and any juices evenly down the center of the uncut portion of the dough. Scatter the chocolate and then the nuts evenly over the figlets.

With a fluted pastry wheel, beginning at the top of the dough, cut thirteen 3¹/2-inch-long diagonal slits 1 inch apart down each side of the square. Starting at the top of the square, alternately bring the left and right strips of dough diagonally over the center of the filling to meet, overlapping them as necessary. Cover the braid with a kitchen towel and let it rest for 40 minutes.

Preheat the oven to 375°F.

Bake the braid for 18 to 20 minutes, until the top and bottom are evenly browned. Let the braid cool on the cookie sheet for about 5 minutes.

continued

Spreading figlets over dough

Spreading nuts and chocolate
centered over figlets

Cutting lattice strips on left and
right sides of dough

Lapping left and right strips
over filling

Braid ready for baking

Meanwhile, in a small bowl, mix the sugar and vanilla with just enough milk to make a smooth glaze. Cover and set aside.

Set a cooling rack over a piece of wax paper. With a spatula, carefully slide the braid onto the rack. With a spoon, drizzle the glaze over the top of the braid. Let the glaze dry, then cut into slices and serve warm or at room temperature.

Poppy Seed Pretzels

Pretzels are always fun to make, especially if they are these sweet poppy seed–filled ones. The sweet dough is first rolled into rustic rounds and filled with a prepared poppy seed filling, then rolled into ropes and shaped into pretzels.

■ MAKES 16 PRETZELS

One 12½-ounce can poppy seed filling
  (such as Solo)
2 tablespoons grated tangerine or orange zest
  (from 2 large tangerines or oranges)
1 recipe Simply Sweet Dough (page 87)
1 egg, beaten with 1 teaspoon half-and-half for
  egg wash

In a bowl, mix the poppy seed filling with the tangerine or orange zest. Set aside.

Lightly spray two baking sheets with vegetable oil spray.

Punch down the dough and turn it out onto a lightly floured work surface. Knead the dough for 3 to 4 minutes, until smooth and no longer sticky. Divide the dough in half. Work with one half at a time, keeping the other half covered with a towel or bowl.

Roll the dough under the palms of your hands into a 12-inch-long log. With a knife, cut the log into eight slices. Roll each slice into a 12- by 4-inch rectangle. Spread 1½ tablespoons of the poppy seed filling evenly over the surface of each piece of dough.

Starting at the long side nearest you, roll up each piece of dough tightly like a jelly roll. Pinch the seam and the two ends closed. Then gently pinch and stretch each piece into a 14-inch-long rope. Bring the two ends together, leaving an inch or so of each free, and twist them twice. Fold the ends over toward the center of the rope to form a rounded pretzel shape, and tuck the ends under.

Place the pretzels 1 inch apart on the prepared baking sheets, cover with a cloth, and let them rise for about 30 minutes.

Preheat the oven to 375°F.

Brush the pretzels with the egg wash. Bake the pretzels for 15 to 18 minutes, until they are nicely

Rolling dough into rectangle

Spreading poppy seed filling
on rectangle

Rolling each piece of dough
like a jelly roll

Pinching dough into a rope

Double twisting pretzel ends

Tucking ends toward the middle

puffed and shiny golden brown. With a spatula, remove the pretzels to a cooling rack.

These are best eaten warm but once cooled, can be frozen, wrapped individually in aluminum foil and then packed in plastic bags. Defrost, unwrapped, at room temperature and reheat in a preheated 325°F oven for 5 minutes.

English Muffins

These English muffins rise like puffy pillows as they cook in a dry hot electric frying pan or a griddle. They have a delicate, subtle sweet taste that goes well with jam or butter. If you'd rather, use half of the dough to make a dozen muffins and turn the remaining half into the wonderful Mango and Dried Cherry Pie (page 115).

■ MAKES 2 DOZEN MUFFINS

1 recipe Simply Sweet Dough (page 87)
Cornmeal for sprinkling

Punch down the dough and and turn it out onto a lightly floured surface. Knead the dough for 3 to 4 minutes, until smooth and no longer sticky. Divide the dough in half and set one half aside, covered with a towel or bowl.

Roll the dough out into a 12-inch circle. Use a 3½-inch round cutter to cut out circles, and place them on a clean kitchen towel. Set the scraps aside and repeat with the remaining dough. Gather the scraps together, roll out, and cut out more circles to make a total of 24.

Cover the dough circles with another towel. Let them rise for 25 minutes.

Preheat an electric skillet to 350°F, or heat a cast-iron griddle. When you are ready to cook the muffins, sprinkle a ½-inch-deep bed of cornmeal over the bottom of the skillet or griddle. Place 4 or 5 of the circles on the cornmeal, spacing them 1 inch apart to allow for expansion. Cook them until nicely browned on the bottom and puffed, about 4 minutes. Turn them over and cook until browned on the other side, 3 to 4 minutes. Remove the muffins to a cooling rack. Repeat the process with the remaining dough circles.

Split the muffins with a fork or a knife, toast, and enjoy. Any leftover muffins can be frozen, well wrapped, for future use.

Fat Tuesday Donuts

On Fat Tuesday, *Martedi Grasso*, the day before the beginning of the long Lenten season, I indulge myself and my family by making these donuts, reminiscent of those I have eaten in Tuscany. Called *bomboloni*, they are usually deep-fried and then given a light veil of confectioners' sugar. In this version, the donuts are baked, then filled with a velvety vanilla and chocolate pastry cream, which gives them a certain culinary panache.

■ MAKES 18 DONUTS

FILLING

1/2 cup granulated sugar
2 large eggs
2 tablespoons unbleached all-purpose flour
1/4 teaspoon salt
2 cups half-and-half
1 tablespoon vanilla extract
2 ounces bittersweet chocolate, finely chopped
Grated zest of 1 large lemon

1 recipe Simply Sweet Dough (page 87)
Confectioners' sugar for sprinkling

In a medium saucepan, off the heat, whisk together the sugar and eggs until smooth. Whisk in the flour 1 tablespoon at a time, then whisk in the salt. Slowly whisk in the half-and-half.

Cook the mixture over medium-low heat, whisking constantly, until the pastry cream thickens enough to coat the back of a spoon, 5 to 7 minutes. Remove the saucepan from the heat and stir in the vanilla.

Pour half the filling into a small bowl. Add the chocolate to the filling remaining in the saucepan and stir until it is completely melted and smooth. Pour the chocolate filling into a small bowl.

Stir half the lemon zest into each bowl of pastry cream. Cover the bowls with plastic wrap, pressing it directly against the surface of the pastry cream, and refrigerate for at least 2 hours.

Lightly spray two baking sheets with vegetable oil spray. Set aside.

Punch down the dough and turn it out onto a floured work surface. Knead for 3 to 4 minutes, until smooth and no longer sticky. Divide the dough in half. Roll each half under your palms into an 18-inch-long rope. Cut each rope into nine 2-inch pieces. Roll each piece into a 2-inch round and space them 1 inch apart on the baking sheets.

Cover the sheets with clean towels and let them rise for 45 minutes, until they double in size.

Preheat the oven to 375°F.

Bake the donuts for 15 to 20 minutes, until golden brown. Remove the donuts to a cooling rack to cool completely.

Fill a 14-inch pastry bag fitted with a 1/2-inch plain tip with the vanilla pastry cream. If you have a second bag and tip, fill it with the chocolate pastry cream. (Or fill half the donuts with the vanilla cream. Then wash and dry the bag and fill the remaining donuts with chocolate cream.)

With the handle of a wooden spoon, carefully make a hole in the side of each donut, twisting the handle gently to bore almost but not quite all the way through the donut.

Insert the tip of one of the pastry bags into one of the prepared holes and squeeze the pastry cream into the donut until the hole is filled. Repeat to fill half the donuts with each flavoring. Place the donuts on a serving dish and sprinkle liberally with confectioners' sugar. (Any leftover pastry cream can be eaten as pudding.)

Note: If you do not have a pastry bag, you can use a large resealable plastic bag. With scissors, cut a small opening in one corner of the bag. Fill the bag with pastry cream, seal the bag, and squeeze the filling into the donuts.

Sunday Coffee Cake

Lazy Sunday mornings often find me slicing warm wedges of this impressive-looking coffee cake filled with walnuts, chocolate, candied orange peel, and crushed *amaretti* cookies. One slice is never enough. This cake makes a great holiday gift from your kitchen. Use a good-quality bitter sweet chocolate, such as Callebout or Lindt. Amaretti cookies can be found in Italian grocery stores and in the gourmet aisle of many supermarkets (or see Mail-Order Sources, page 143). ■ MAKES ONE 9-INCH COFFEE CAKE; SERVES 8 TO 10

3/4 cup crumbled amaretti cookies (10 to 12 cookies)
1 cup finely chopped walnuts
4 ounces bittersweet chocolate, finely chopped
1/2 cup diced homemade (page 135) or storebought candied orange peel
1 recipe Simply Sweet Dough (page 87)
1 tablespoon milk

GLAZE
1 cup confectioners' sugar
1/4 teaspoon almond extract
1 1/2 to 2 tablespoons milk or half-and-half

Brush a 9- by 2¼-inch ring mold with butter and set aside.

Combine the cookies, walnuts, chocolate, and orange peel in a bowl and set aside.

Punch down the dough and turn it out onto a lightly floured surface. Knead the dough for 3 to 4 minutes, until smooth and no longer sticky. Roll it out to an 18-inch round.

Brush the dough with the milk. Spread the filling mixture evenly over the surface, pressing the mixture gently into the dough and leaving a ½-inch border all around. Roll the dough up tightly like a jelly roll. Seal the seam by pinching it together. With the palms of your hands, gently roll the dough into a 21-inch-long log.

Place the log, seam side down, in the ring mold. Pinch the two ends together to seal them. Cover the pan with a clean cloth and let rise in a warm place for 45 minutes.

Preheat the oven to 375°F.

Bake the coffee cake for 40 to 50 minutes, until the top is nicely browned and a cake skewer inserted in the cake comes out clean. Cool the cake in the ring pan on a rack for 10 minutes.

Meanwhile, make the glaze. In a small bowl, combine the sugar and almond extract with just enough milk to make a smooth glaze. Run a table knife around the edges of the ring mold. Carefully invert the cake onto the cooling rack. Turn the coffee cake right side up, and place a sheet of wax paper under the rack. Spoon the warm glaze over the top of the coffee cake, letting the excess drip down the sides. Cut into slices and serve warm, or let cool to room temperature.

Plum Kuchen

Glistening slices of scarlet red plums soaked in sweet Marsala wine snuggle together atop this wonderful kuchen, which will please a crowd at brunch or afternoon tea. To have the kuchen warm and waiting for friends, macerate the plums a day ahead and refrigerate. Make the dough, let it rise until almost doubled in size, place it in a plastic bag, and refrigerate it. The next morning, put the dough in a bowl and let it come to room temperature and rise again, then assemble the kuchen and bake.

■ SERVES 16 TO 20

2 pounds red or purple plums (10 medium),
   halved, pitted, and cut into $1/4$-inch-thick slices
$1/3$ cup sweet Marsala wine
2 tablespoons unsalted butter, melted
Grated zest of 1 large lemon
1 recipe Simply Sweet Dough (page 87)
$1/4$ cup currant jelly, melted

Place the plums in a large shallow glass dish and pour the wine over them. Gently toss the slices in the wine with a spoon. Cover the dish and let the plums macerate for at least several hours, or overnight.

Lightly brush a $17\frac{1}{2}$- by $11\frac{1}{2}$-inch baking pan with 1 tablespoon of the melted butter and set aside.

Dust a work surface lightly with flour and sprinkle the lemon zest over the flour. Punch down the dough and turn it out onto the work surface. Knead the dough for 3 to 4 minutes, until smooth and no longer sticky, evenly incorporating the zest as you knead.

Roll the dough out into an 18- by 14-inch rectangle and fit it into the baking pan, bringing the dough up along the sides and fitting it into the pan. Brush the dough with the remaining melted butter.

Drain the plum slices, reserving the wine.

Make seven or eight overlapping lengthwise rows of plum slices on top of the dough, pressing the slices slightly into the dough. Drizzle the reserved wine over the top of the slices. Cover the kuchen with a clean towel and let it rise for 30 minutes.

Preheat the oven to 375°F.

Bake the kuchen on the middle oven rack for 30 to 35 minutes, until the edges of the dough have browned and a knife inserted into the center of the kuchen comes out clean.

Remove the kuchen to a rack. With a pastry brush, glaze the top of the kuchen with the melted jelly. Let the kuchen cool slightly, then cut it into squares and serve warm.

Sicilian Ice Cream Cones

This recipe was inspired by an afternoon of people watching one glorious spring day in Sicily. I sat in the piazza of the seaside resort of Mondello, watching the colored fishing boats and the fishermen busy with their catch. People of all ages meandered by my table, munching on biscotti and intriguing-looking cone-shaped rolls stuffed with ice cream, the most beloved Sicilian treat. These rolls are fun to make, and a great conversation piece. You will need cone-shaped metal molds, called cream horn forms, for this recipe (see Mail-Order Sources, page 143); if you have eighteen molds, you can bake the cones in just two batches. The cones can be frozen, and they are great for a party. Fill them with sorbet or pudding too!

■ MAKES 36 CONES

1 recipe Simply Sweet Dough (page 87)
1 large egg, slightly beaten

Preheat the oven to 375°F. Lightly spray eighteen 4½-inch metal pastry cones with vegetable oil spray. Line two baking sheets with parchment paper.

Punch down the dough and turn it out onto a lightly floured work surface. Knead the dough for 3 to 4 minutes, until smooth and no longer sticky. Divide the dough in half and work with one half of the dough at a time, keeping the second half covered with a towel or bowl.

Roll the dough out under the palms of your hands into an 18-inch-long rope. With a knife, cut it into eighteen 1-inch pieces. Roll each piece out with a rolling pin into a 7- by 2¼-inch strip. Wrap each strip around a lightly sprayed pastry cone, starting just below the rim of the top edge of the cone and working down to the tapered point, overlapping the edges slightly as you go. Brush the end of each strip with a little of the beaten egg and press firmly to seal the tapered end of the cone.

Place the cones on the parchment-lined baking sheets, spacing them 1 inch apart.

Bake the cones for about 20 minutes, until they are golden brown. Carefully transfer the cones to a cooling rack. When they are cool to the touch, gently twist the pastry cones to release them and remove. Repeat the process with the remaining dough.

Just before serving, fill the cones with your favorite ice cream. Or let people fill their own.

To freeze, wrap each cone in plastic wrap, then place in freezer bags.

Sweet Spiral Wreath

Who says you can't make two things at once? For a company Sunday brunch, I like to use half the Simply Sweet Dough to make the luscious Fig, Chocolate, and Walnut Braid (page 97) and half to make this sugared spiral wreath. The only problem is which to eat first. Using a perforated pizza pan allows for even baking of the bottom of the wreath and helps to align the spirals for the finished look. ■ MAKES 1 WREATH

1/2 recipe Simply Sweet Dough (page 87)
1 egg, slightly beaten
2 tablespoons turbinado (coarse brown) sugar

Lightly spray a 16-inch perforated pizza pan or a baking sheet with vegetable oil spray and set aside.

Punch down the dough and turn it out onto a lightly floured work surface. Knead it for 3 to 4 minutes, until smooth and no longer sticky. Roll the dough into a 12- by 9-inch rectangle.

Using a pastry wheel, cut it crosswise into twelve 1-inch-wide strips.

Roll up each of 11 of the strips into a tight spiral, leaving about a 2-inch-long tail. Arrange the spirals close together—they should just touch one other—in a circle on the pizza pan or baking sheet, with their tails toward the center. Roll the last strip into a tight spiral and place it in the middle of the circle.

Cover the spirals with a kitchen towel and let them rise for 40 minutes, until almost doubled in size.

Preheat the oven to 375°F.

Brush the spirals with the beaten egg and sprinkle the turbinado sugar evenly over the tops. Bake for 18 to 20 minutes, until the wreath is golden brown on the top and bottom.

Let the wreath cool in the pan for 10 minutes. With a metal spatula, carefully slide the wreath onto a cooling rack. Pull apart to serve.

Mango and Dried Cherry Pie

Here's a refreshing change from the traditional two-crusted pie—an open-faced, free-form one filled with fresh mango and dried cherries. The glistening sweet-and-tart combination makes a delicious filling for this shimmering, jewel-like dessert. Want two pies? Double the filling ingredients and use the full recipe of Simply Sweet Dough. ■ MAKES ONE 10-INCH PIE; SERVES 8

1 cup dried cherries
1/4 cup amaretto liqueur
1/2 recipe Simply Sweet Dough (page 87)
1 large mango, peeled, seeded, and diced
1 egg, slightly beaten
1 tablespoon turbinado (coarse brown) sugar

Place the cherries in a small bowl and pour the liqueur over them. Stir well and let macerate for at least 1 hour.

Butter a 10- by 2-inch round baking dish, or spray with vegetable oil spray, and set aside.

Punch down the dough and turn it out onto a lightly floured surface. Knead it for 3 to 4 minutes, until smooth and no longer sticky.

Roll the dough out into a 15-inch circle. Carefully lift the dough up and place it in the baking dish, letting the excess overhang the sides of the dish.

Add the mango pieces to the cherries and spread the fruit, with its liquid, over the dough.

Using scissors, cut 2-inch slits in the overhanging dough all around the dish. Fold the dough over the filling, leaving the center exposed. Cover the dish with a towel and let the pie rise for 35 minutes.

Preheat the oven to 375°F.

Brush the top of the dough with the beaten egg and sprinkle the sugar over it. Bake the pie for 30 to 35 minutes, until it is golden brown and firm to the touch. Cool the pie completely in the baking dish.

Cut the pie into wedges to serve. Or, to remove the entire pie from the dish, run a table knife around the edges of the dish and with a spatula, carefully lift the pie onto a serving plate.

Almond Paste Holiday Bread

For these elegant and wonderfully scented almond breads, use a good commercially prepared almond paste, such as Solo, or make your own. Almond paste can be stored in the refrigerator for weeks or in the freezer for months. Jam can be used in place of almond paste, as can ground walnuts and raisins.

■ MAKES 2 LOAVES

1 recipe Simply Sweet Dough (page 87)
3 cups almond paste, homemade (page 134) or store-bought
1 egg, slightly beaten with 1 tablespoon water for egg wash

GLAZE
1½ cups confectioners' sugar
½ teaspoon almond extract
3 to 4 tablespoons milk or half-and-half

Lightly spray two baking sheets with vegetable oil spray.

Punch down the dough and turn it out onto a lightly floured surface. Knead for 3 to 4 minutes, until smooth and no longer sticky. Divide the dough in half and cover one half with a towel or bowl.

Roll out the other piece of dough to an 18-inch round. Spread 1½ cups of the almond paste evenly over the dough to within ¼ inch of the edges. Starting at the edge nearest you, roll the dough up tightly like a jelly roll, tucking in the ends as you roll. Punch the seam closed and put the dough seam side down on one of the prepared baking sheets. Shape the dough into a candy cane, wreath, or S shape; if you've made a wreath, pinch the ends of the dough together and tuck them under to seal the seam. Cover with a clean towel and let the dough rise for 45 minutes.

Repeat with the remaining dough and almond paste.

Preheat the oven to 375°F.

Brush the tops of each bread with the egg wash. With scissors, make a few decorative slashes lengthwise down the center of the candy cane shape, or cut ½-inch slashes about 1 inch apart around the edges of the wreath or the S shape. Bake for 35 to 40 minutes, until the breads are a rich brown on both the top and bottom. Cool the breads on wire racks until just warm.

Meanwhile, in a bowl, mix the confectioners' sugar with the almond extract and just enough of the milk to make a smooth glaze. The glaze should be just thick enough to flow slowly off a spoon.

With a spoon, drizzle the glaze over the warm breads. Let the glaze dry completely. Serve the breads warm or at room temperature. The breads can be frozen, well wrapped in heavy-duty aluminum foil and then in plastic bags, for up to 2 months.

Beyond Bread Crumbs

■

It seems so unforgivable to waste bread and yet each day many of us just toss out those unyielding hard heels of the loaf or other stale bread pieces without realizing what potential there is in leftover bread. I would do this book and you, the reader, a disservice if I did not include recipes for "forgotten bread."

In Europe, and especially in Italy, bread has a sacredness about it, a special status, because of its historic symbolism as the most basic of human food. Many of us have never known what it is to want for bread, or in a more universal sense, want for food. This chapter offers you recipes made from both plain and sweet leftover bread. They were born out of a need in the past to "stretch" a meal in order to make it go farther. I think you will find that the recipes in this chapter created with bread are worthy enough to challenge any "gourmet" dish.

Of course the most common use for leftover bread is for making bread crumbs. In Italian cooking, both plain bread crumbs and sweet bread crumbs are used not only in recipes but also for coating cake pans and molds. Sweet crumbs are often mixed into cake and cookie batters; they are liberally sprinkled on top of mousses and puddings; and I have even seen bananas coated in chocolate and rolled in toasted bread crumbs for a delicious treat. A common use for plain bread crumbs is as a seasoned stuffing for vegetables and meats or as the coating for chicken and veal cutlets.

In this chapter you will find other uses for leftover bread, including unusual bread salads, my mother's bread stuffing for poultry, and a warm and comforting bread pudding, but these are just the starting point for giving new life to tired old bread.

Homemade Bread Crumbs

The best bread crumbs can only be made with stale homemade bread. Save the heels of loaves of bread, trimmed-off crusts, or just forgotten bread in a paper bag. Plain white bread makes the best all-purpose bread crumbs, but whole wheat, rye, and pumpernickel can be put to good use in recipes as well and offer taste variations. When you have enough to warrant turning on the oven, place the bread pieces on a cookie sheet and toast in a 300°F oven until they are dry and hard. Let the pieces cool, then put them in a large paper bag or heavy-duty plastic bag and fold over the open end of the paper bag and tape it closed, or seal the plastic bag. Roll over the bag several times with a rolling pin until the bread is reduced to crumbs—control the fineness of the crumbs by the amount of rolling. Or use a food processor to pulverize the bread. Store the bread crumbs in glass jars or plastic containers in the refrigerator and use as needed. Make flavored bread crumbs by adding herbs, salt and pepper, or even grated cheese and hot pepper flakes.

You can make bread crumbs from sweet breads in exactly the same way. One of my favorite uses for bread crumbs from leftover sweet bread is as a coating for cake pans, bread pans, and molds. ■ MAKES 2 CUPS

1/4 cup extra-virgin olive oil
3 tablespoons unsalted butter
2 cups bread crumbs
Fine sea salt to taste
Coarsely ground black pepper to taste (optional)

In a skillet, heat the oil and butter and mix well. Add the bread crumbs and stir constantly with a wooden spoon until the crumbs absorb all the oil-butter mixture and are golden brown. Season with salt and with pepper if desired, and remove the crumbs to a bowl. When cool, transfer the crumbs to an airtight container and store in the refrigerator. They will keep for several months.

Variation: Add minced fresh herbs such as parsley, oregano, and/or basil to the cooled crumbs. Bread crumbs containing herbs should be used within a week.

Grated cheeses, such as Parmigiano-Reggiano, Pecorino, and Swiss, can also be added to bread crumbs, along with some hot red pepper flakes if you'd like.

Bread Pudding

Use leftover bread from recipes using the Simply Sweet Dough (page 87) to make this delicious and comforting bread pudding. It is a great fall and wintertime dessert and a great way to use up leftover holiday breads. (If you don't have any leftover sweet bread, you can use plain bread, but increase the sugar to three quarters of a cup.)

■ SERVES 8 TO 10

5 cups 1-inch pieces stale sweet bread
$^1/_2$ cup sweet Marsala wine
4 cups milk
$^1/_2$ cup light cream or half-and-half
$^1/_2$ teaspoon ground cinnamon
$^1/_2$ teaspoon grated nutmeg
1 tablespoon grated lemon zest
1 tablespoon grated orange zest
4 large eggs, separated
$^1/_3$ cup sugar
Whipped cream or vanilla ice cream for serving

Preheat the oven to 325°F. Butter a 9- by 12-inch baking dish.

Put the bread in a large bowl, add the Marsala wine, and toss until the bread is evenly moistened. Set aside.

Bring the milk and cream to a boil in a large saucepan. Remove from the heat and stir in the cinnamon, nutmeg, and lemon and orange zests.

In a large bowl, whisk the egg yolks until light and fluffy; whisk in the cream mixture. In another large bowl, beat the egg whites until stiff but not dry. Add the sugar. Fold into the bread mixture. Pour the mixture into the prepared dish. Place the dish in a large baking pan and carefully add hot water to come halfway up the sides of the baking dish. Bake the pudding until a knife inserted in the custard comes out clean, about 2 hours.

Serve the bread pudding warm, with a garnish of whipped cream or a small scoop of vanilla ice cream.

Crunchy Croutons

Cubes of stale bread can be used to make home-made croutons. I like to prepare a mixture of different kinds of croutons made from rye, oat, wheat, and white breads. Buttered croutons have the best flavor, but you can toast them dry for a low-fat alternative to the buttery ones. Store croutons in glass or plastic containers in the refrigerator and sprinkle them on soups, toss into salads, and use in stuffings for all kinds of fowl, beef, pork, fish, and vegetables. For flavored croutons for salads and soups, toss them with a mixture of olive oil, grated cheese, and minced herbs.

■ MAKES 4 CUPS

8 tablespoons (1 stick) unsalted butter, melted
4 cups 1/2-inch cubes stale bread, preferably
    several different kinds

Preheat the oven to 325°F.

Pour the melted butter into a medium bowl. Add the bread and toss to coat with the butter. Spread the bread on a baking sheet.

Bake for 25 to 30 minutes, until the croutons are hard and golden brown. Cool on the baking sheet, then store in airtight containers in the refrigerator for up to 3 weeks.

Note: To make flavored croutons, toss the bread and butter mixture with 2 tablespoons of your favorite minced herbs, 2 tablespoons freshly grated Parmigiano-Reggiano cheese, and salt and pepper to taste. Bake as directed.

Gnocchi di Pane/Bread Gnocchi

Say "gnocchi" to any Italian cook and invariably you will get many explanations as to what they are. Many consider gnocchi only to be little dumplings made with potato and flour, but there are many variations of gnocchi, based on ingredients from semolina to ricotta. These bread gnocchi are made with day-old bread, eggs, flour, and cheese. They are delicious served with a sauce of butter, garlic, and parsley.

■ MAKES ABOUT 5 DOZEN GNOCCHI; SERVES 10

DOUGH
2 cups finely crumbled crustless bread
1 1/4 cups milk
1 large egg
1/2 cup freshly grated Parmigiano-Reggiano
    cheese
1 teaspoon fine sea salt
1 3/4 to 2 cups unbleached all-purpose flour

SAUCE
8 tablespoons (1 stick) unsalted butter
1 large clove garlic, thinly sliced
1/2 cup finely minced fresh flat-leaf parsley

Place the bread in a bowl, add the milk, egg, cheese, and salt and mix well. Add just enough flour to make a thick dough (too much flour will make the dumplings heavy) and knead it until it is the consistency of mashed potatoes. Cover the bowl with plastic wrap and refrigerate for 1 1/2 hours.

Bring 3 quarts of salted water to the boil in a large pot. Preheat the oven to 200°F. Butter a large casserole dish with 1 tablespoon of the butter.

Meanwhile, in a medium saucepan, melt the remaining 7 tablespoons butter. Add the garlic and cook for about 1 minute, pressing on it with a wooden spoon to flavor the butter. Discard the gar-

lic, add the parsley, and cook until the butter browns slightly. Keep the sauce warm over very low heat.

Using two teaspoons dipped in ice water, drop small spoonfuls of the dough into the boiling water, about 2 dozen at a time. Once the gnocchi bob to the top, cook until just tender, about 5 minutes longer. Remove with a slotted spoon, draining them well, and place in the casserole dish. Keep warm in the oven while you cook the remaining gnocchi.

Pour the butter sauce over the gnocchi, toss gently with a spoon to coat them evenly, and serve immediately.

Sailor-Style Bread Salad

Here is another example of getting new life from leftover bread. This bread and tuna salad was originally a clever use of stale bread by Italian sailors, who combined it with the fish they caught at sea, a few spices, and olive oil. Consider this lively salad, with its pungent capers, olives, and anchovies, a meal in itself. Make it early in the day to allow the flavors to soak into the bread. ■ SERVES 6 TO 8

Two 6 1/2-ounce cans tuna in olive oil

4 cups stale bread chunks

4 shallots, finely minced

One 4-ounce can anchovies in olive oil, drained and cut into small pieces, oil reserved

1/2 cup finely chopped oil-cured black olives

1/2 cup extra-virgin olive oil

1 tablespoon capers in brine, drained and minced

1 tablespoon minced fresh oregano or 1 teaspoon dried

Fine sea salt to taste

1/2 teaspoon coarsely ground black pepper

1 lemon, thinly sliced

1 orange, thinly sliced

Drain the tuna, reserving the olive oil. Place the tuna in a small bowl, flake it with a fork, and set aside.

Fill a large bowl with cool water. Quickly dip the bread chunks into the water to moisten them. Squeeze the bread dry and crumble it onto a large serving platter.

In a medium bowl, mix the shallots, anchovies and their oil, the tuna oil, olives, 1/3 cup of the extra-virgin olive oil, the capers, oregano, salt, and pepper. Mix in the tuna. Pour this mixture over the bread and toss to combine well. Drizzle the remaining olive oil over the top.

Arrange the lemon and orange slices around the edges of the platter, overlapping them slightly. Cover the platter tightly with plastic wrap and let sit at room temperature for 2 to 3 hours before serving. (Or refrigerate for longer, but bring to room temperature before serving.)

Panzanella/Bread Salad

Wet bread does not sound appetizing, but when it becomes *panzanella*, also called *insalata di pan-bagnato*, a salad made with stale bread moistened in water and combined with raw summer vegetables and a vinaigrette, stale bread becomes, in a word, refreshing. It is best to make this salad early in the day to allow the bread to absorb the flavors of the other ingredients. Be sure to use a coarse-textured country-type bread such as Pane Casereccio (page 22); spongy supermarket white bread will just disintegrate when moistened.

■ SERVES 6

1 cup coarsely chopped plum or cherry tomatoes
1 teaspoon sugar
6 slices stale bread
1/2 cup thinly sliced red onions
1/2 cup seeded and diced sweet green pepper
1/2 cup diced fennel bulb
1 cup seeded and diced cucumber
2 tablespoons capers in brine, drained and minced
1/4 cup minced fresh flat-leaf parsley
2 tablespoons minced fresh basil

DRESSING
6 tablespoons extra-virgin olive oil
3 tablespoons red wine vinegar
2 cloves garlic, minced
Fine sea salt and coarsely ground black pepper
    to taste

Place the tomatoes in a small bowl, stir in the sugar, and set aside.

Dip the pieces of bread in a bowl of water, making sure to moisten them thoroughly. Squeeze out the excess water with your hands and crumble the bread into bite-size pieces into a salad bowl. Add all the remaining salad ingredients, including the tomatoes.

Combine the dressing ingredients in a small jar, cover, and shake well. Pour the dressing over the salad and gently toss to combine well. Cover the bowl with plastic wrap and let the salad macerate at room temperature for several hours before serving.

Louisa's Bread Stuffing

One of the popular uses for leftover bread is for bread stuffing. This is my mother's standard recipe, which she uses to stuff chicken, turkey, and capon. ■ SERVES 4 TO 6

STUFFING
2 tablespoons butter
$1/2$ cup chopped onions
$1^1/2$ cups chopped celery
Salt and coarsely ground black pepper to taste
$1/2$ cup dark raisins
$1^1/2$ cups $1/2$-inch cubes stale bread
$1/2$ cup chicken broth

One 4-pound roasting chicken, rinsed and dried
Salt and coarsely ground black pepper to taste
2 tablespoons butter, melted

In a medium skillet, melt the butter. Add the onions and celery and cook until translucent. Season with salt and pepper. Add the raisins and cook 1 minute longer. Set aside.

Place the bread cubes in a large bowl and moisten them with the broth. Gently stir in the onion and celery mixture. Let cool.

Preheat the oven to 350°F.

Season the cavity of the chicken with salt and pepper. Stuff the cavity loosely with the bread mixture, and sew the cavity closed with butcher's twine or skewer it closed if desired. Baste the chicken all over with the melted butter. Place on a rack in a roasting pan, breast side up.

Roast the chicken, basting occasionally with the pan drippings, for about $1^1/2$ hours, until the juices from the thigh run clear when it is pierced. Remove the chicken to a cutting board and let it cool for 10 minutes.

With a large spoon, scoop the stuffing from the cavity into a serving bowl. Cover to keep the stuffing warm while you carve the chicken. Serve immediately.

Grated Pasta/Pasta Grattata

These unusual shaggy-looking noodles are called *pasta grattata* because they are formed using a cheese grater. Bread crumbs give texture and structure to the dough, which must be chilled overnight to make it easier to grate. The pasta is traditionally served in clear chicken or beef broth. ▪ SERVES 8 TO 10

1 cup toasted fresh bread crumbs
³/₄ cup freshly grated Parmigiano-Reggiano
   cheese
¹/₂ cup plus 2 tablespoons unbleached all-purpose
   flour
Grated zest of 1 medium lemon
1¹/₂ teaspoons fresh lemon juice
2 large eggs, slightly beaten
Fine sea salt and coarsely ground black pepper
   to taste
4 quarts chicken or beef broth

In a large bowl, mix the bread crumbs, cheese, and flour together. In another bowl, mix the remaining ingredients, except the broth, together. Add to the flour mixture and mix well with your hands. Gather the dough—it will be rough look-ing—into a ball. Wrap the dough in plastic wrap and refrigerate for at least 6 to 7 hours or overnight.

Place a sheet of parchment paper on a work surface. Using the large holes of a box grater, grate the pasta onto the paper, spreading the pasta out on the paper as you work.

In a large pot, bring the broth to a boil. Add the pasta and boil for about 5 minutes, or until the pasta floats to the surface. Ladle the soup into bowls and serve immediately.

Note: To freeze for future use, spread the uncooked pasta out on a floured baking sheet and freeze until hard. Transfer the pasta to airtight plastic bags and freeze. Do not defrost before cooking.

Adding cheese to the
bread crumbs

Adding liquids to the dry
ingredients

Mixing the dough by hand

Ball of dough

Grating the chilled
ball of dough

Grated pasta

Soup with Bread Under It

In ancient times, bread and bread crumbs were often used to thicken soups and sauces. One of my favorite soups is a traditional bread soup combined with bitter greens. Stale bread is used to thicken the soup as well as make it go farther. This is sometimes referred to as *zuppa contadina* (peasant soup). ■ SERVES 8 TO 10

1/4 cup extra-virgin olive oil
1 medium onion, thinly sliced
1 cup thinly sliced celery
2 cloves garlic, minced
8 cups chopped tomatoes (about 5 pounds)
3 sprigs fresh basil
Fine sea salt and coarsely ground black pepper to taste
1 pound Swiss chard or spinach, stemmed and washed
Twelve 1-inch-thick slices day-old or stale bread
1/2 cup freshly grated Pecorino Romano cheese

Heat the olive oil in a large soup pot over medium heat. Add the onion and celery and cook for 5 minutes. Add the garlic and cook until the garlic is soft but not browned. Add the tomatoes, basil, and salt and pepper. Stir well and simmer, covered, for 20 minutes.

Meanwhile, bring a large pot of water to a boil. Add the Swiss chard or spinach and boil for 3 to 4 minutes. Drain well.

Coarsely chop the chard or spinach and add it to the soup. Stir well and simmer for 10 minutes.

Place a layer of bread slices in a deep platter. Spread just enough of the soup over the bread to cover it. Sprinkle with some of the cheese. Make a second layer of bread, soup, and cheese, and continue layering until all the bread and soup are used. Serve immediately.

Lemony Mashed Potatoes

Because I make Nonna's Sponge Dough so often, mashed potatoes are a frequent part of our meals. I prefer to use all-purpose potatoes but the choice is yours. Do not choose baking potatoes, however, which tend to be drier in texture. I also like to mash potatoes with a hand masher, not with an electric mixer. Don't use a food processor—it tends to make the potatoes gummy.

■ SERVES 4 TO 6

1½ pounds all-purpose potatoes, peeled and quartered
5 cups filtered or bottled noncarbonated water
3 tablespoons butter, melted
1½ teaspoons fine sea salt
5 tablespoons half-and-half or milk
Grated zest of 1 medium lemon
1 tablespoon fresh lemon juice

Place the potatoes in a medium saucepan and pour in the water. Bring to a boil and cook the potatoes for 10 to 12 minutes, or until easily pierced with a knife. Drain the potatoes in a colander set over a bowl. Refrigerate or freeze the water to use for Nonna's Sponge Dough (page 59).

Transfer the potatoes to a medium bowl and mash them with the butter and salt until smooth. Add the half-and-half or milk and continue mashing until all the liquid has been absorbed. Stir in the lemon zest and juice. Serve immediately, with additional butter if you wish.

Homemade Is Better

■

I am one of those "from-scratch" cooks who take great pleasure in having on hand some favorite staple ingredients that they've made themselves. I just don't have it in me to purchase commercially prepared foods such as almond paste or eggplant caponata when I know I can easily make these at home for a fraction of the cost. I also have the comfort of knowing that what I make from scratch is free of artificial flavorings or preservatives—and it will taste wonderful.

All of the homemade ingredients in this chapter are used in at least one of the other recipes in this book, but don't let that limit your use of them. They can be used in many other preparations as well, and they also make a welcome gift from your kitchen.

Almond Paste

Almond paste is one of my staple fillings for sweet breads, rolls, tarts, and cookies. Use it for the Almond Paste Holiday Bread on page 116.

■ MAKES 1¾ POUNDS

1 pound slivered blanched almonds
3 cups confectioners' sugar
2 large egg whites
2 tablespoons water
1 teaspoon almond extract
Pinch of salt

Grind the almonds to a powder in a food processor or blender. Add the sugar and blend well. With the motor running, add the remaining ingredients and process until a smooth paste is formed. Transfer the almond paste to clean jars and refrigerate, or freeze for up to 3 months.

Candied Orange Peel

Candied fruit peels are staple ingredients in the Italian kitchen and are used in many sweet yeast breads, cakes, and cookies. Holiday breads including such regional specialties as *panettone, panforte,* and *gubana* sparkle with candied orange and lemon peel. Finding good candied citrus peel can sometimes be difficult. Although it is found in some Italian specialty stores year round, it is most readily available at holiday time; you can buy it then in bulk and freeze it. But if you make your own candied fruit peels, you can have a ready supply, and the process is quite simple. Orange, lemon, tangerine, and even grapefruit peels all can be successfully candied, but it is important to remove the bitter pith, the white part of the peel.

My favorite is orange peel, and I encourage you to try this basic recipe. Be sure to use coarse turbinado sugar for the final coating of the cooked peel; it doesn't melt or dissolve as readily as regular granular sugar. Candied citrus peel looks very attractive stored in a glass jar—give it as a gift from your kitchen.

■ MAKES ABOUT 2 CUPS

3 large navel oranges, washed
1 1/2 cups water
1 1/4 cups granulated sugar
1/4 teaspoon salt
2/3 cup turbinado (coarse brown) sugar

Cut the oranges in half and squeeze the juice; you should have about 1 cup. Set the juice aside. Cut each orange half in two and pull out the pulp and membranes. Using a very sharp small knife, scrape away most of the white pith from the peel and discard it. Cut the orange peel into 1/4-inch-wide strips. (Do not worry if the strips are not the same length.) Place the strips in a medium saucepan and cover with 2 1/2 cups of cold water. Bring to a boil and boil for 1 minute. Drain the peel and rinse the saucepan. Repeat the process two times. Set the drained peel aside. (Blanching the peel in boiling water helps to eliminate the bitterness.)

Pour the orange juice into a medium saucepan and add the water, granulated sugar, and salt. Bring to a boil, stirring to dissolve the sugar. Add the orange peel and stir the ingredients with a wooden spoon. Lower the heat and simmer, uncovered, for about 2 1/2 hours, until the syrup thickens and reduces by about two thirds; it should be the consistency of corn syrup.

Spread the turbinado sugar in a 9- by 12-inch baking pan. Line a baking sheet with wax paper.

With a slotted spoon, remove the peel from the syrup and spread it over the turbinado sugar. With your fingers, roll the strips in the sugar to coat them evenly on all sides. Place the sugared strips on the baking sheet and let them dry, uncovered, overnight.

Store the candied peel in glass jars in the refrigerator or in glass jars or Ziploc bags in the freezer. Either way, they will last for months.

Variation: You can make candied lemon peel in the same way, using 4 large lemons. Increase the amount of granulated sugar to 1 1/2 cups.

Vanilla Extract

Most supermarkets carry pure vanilla extract, and there are excellent vanillas available by mail order (see page 143), but it is very simple to make your own. You only need two ingredients, alcohol and vanilla beans. ∎ MAKES 1 CUP

1 vanilla bean
1 cup brandy or dark rum

With a small knife, cut the vanilla bean in half, then slit each half lengthwise. Put the pieces in a clean glass jar and add the brandy or rum. Cap the jar and store it in a cool, dark place for at least 6 weeks to allow the flavor to develop.

Strain the extract through a cheesecloth-lined strainer into a decorative bottle. Cap and keep on your pantry shelf. The vanilla will continue to mature in the bottle.

Spicy Mustard

If you are a spicy mustard fan, you owe it to
yourself to try this easy recipe. You'll find it
becomes one of your must-have-on-hand
ingredients. Use it for Spicy Mustard, Potato, and
Red Onion Pizza (page 45). Slather it on Braided
Sesame Bread (page 23) and add your favorite
sandwich filling. Dip Grissini Rustici (page 25)
into it. Top dainty pieces of cheese with it for an
antipasto, or use it in sauces and marinades.

■ MAKES 3 PINTS

1 cup brown mustard seeds
1 cup yellow mustard seeds
2 cups red wine vinegar
$1/2$ cup honey
2 teaspoons fine sea salt
1 teaspoon ground allspice
6 sterilized $1/2$-pint jars

Put the mustard seeds in a noncorrosive large
bowl and pour the vinegar over them. Cover the
bowl tightly with plastic wrap and let the seeds
soak for 2 days. As they do, they will absorb the
vinegar.

Transfer the mustard seeds to a food processor.
Add the honey, salt, and allspice and pulse until a
grainy paste is formed. (If you want a smoother
texture, pulse longer.)

Fill the jars with the mustard. Place a round of
wax paper slightly larger than the jar opening over
the top of each one and cap. Store in the refrigerator for up to 3 months.

Dried Tomatoes in Olive Oil

Some foods go in and out of fashion, but dried tomatoes in olive oil are here to stay. Although they are often called "sun-dried," most are produced with no sun at all. I like to use a dehydrator, but you can also dry the tomatoes in a low oven. Drying the tomatoes really concentrates the flavor. Dried tomatoes are wonderful flavor enhancements for many recipes. Like Tangy Tomato Logs (page 33), the best dried tomatoes come from ripe tomatoes in season, and I think the best ones to dry are Roma plum tomatoes. Cherry tomatoes work well too. Keep several jars of these tomatoes on hand to add to your favorite recipes. ■ MAKES 3 CUPS

14 unblemished, plump plum tomatoes
3 cups red wine vinegar
8 fresh basil leaves
3 tablespoons capers in brine, drained
2 tablespoons black peppercorns
2 teaspoons fine sea salt
2 to 2$^1/_2$ cups extra-virgin olive oil
2 sterilized 12-ounce jars

Wash and dry the tomatoes. Core and cut them lengthwise in half. Place cut sides down in a dehydrator and dry according to the manufacturer's instructions. Or place cut sides down on wire racks on baking sheets, place in a preheated 225°F oven, and let them dry until they have the texture of dried apricots; this may take a day or two, depending on the size of the tomatoes.

Pour the wine vinegar into a large noncorrosive saucepan and bring to a boil. Add the tomatoes and blanch them for 1 minute. Remove the tomatoes with a slotted spoon and drain well.

Layer the tomatoes into the sterilized jars, adding half the basil, capers, peppercorns, and salt to each jar. Slowly pour the olive oil into the jars, pressing down on the tomatoes slightly with a wooden spoon. Make sure the tomatoes are completely submerged under the oil or they will be exposed to the air and potential bacteria. Cap the jars and place them in a cool spot overnight.

Add more oil to the jars if the tomatoes are poking out of the oil. Check the jars two or three more times over the next day or so, adding more oil if necessary.

Cap the jars and store them in a cool place for 6 weeks before using. Refrigerate after opening, and bring the tomatoes to room temperature before using.

Quick Tomato Sauce

There is no reason to resort to using jarred tomato sauce when it is so simple to make your own, and the taste comparisons are like night and day. So how do you have homemade tomato sauce on hand every time you need it? Simple. Make it when tomatoes are at their best and freeze the sauce in heavy-duty plastic bags. This recipe is very basic and can be prepared in short order. ▪ MAKES 4 CUPS

1/4 cup olive oil
3 cloves garlic, finely chopped
4 cups coarsely chopped fresh plum tomatoes
    (about 8 medium tomatoes), drained
1 1/2 tablespoons chopped fresh oregano or
    1 tablespoon dried
2 teaspoons fine sea salt
1/4 cup chopped fresh basil

In a large saucepan, heat the oil over medium heat. Sauté the garlic until soft. Add the tomatoes, oregano, and salt. Simmer over low heat for about 15 minutes, until slightly thickened. Remove from the heat and stir in the basil.

Variation: If you prefer a smoother sauce, puree the tomatoes in a food processor or food mill before adding to the saucepan.

Caponata

Caponata encapsulates the very history of Sicilian foods. In its ingredients and preparation, I can find the influence of the Greeks, who introduced pungent capers, and their love of olives; the Arabs, who combined their fondness for sugar with eggplant, vinegar, and onions to produce what became the Sicilian flavor known as *agrodolce* (sweet-and-sour); and the Spaniards, who introduced the use of cocoa into the cooking of the island. Eggplant caponata is one of the classic dishes of Sicily, and the most popular, but there are many versions of caponata that do not use eggplant at all; some are made with stale bread, anchovies, and tuna, others with almonds and artichokes. This recipe is used for the filling for the Caponata Tartlets on page 74, but it is equally good served as a spread for homemade bread, stirred into cooked rice, or used as a quick sauce for pasta. ■ MAKES ABOUT 9½ CUPS

8 small eggplants (4 to 5 inches long), cut into
    1-inch chunks
Coarse salt
1½ cups water
1¼ cups thinly sliced celery
About 1½ cups peanut oil
½ cup extra-virgin olive oil
4 medium onions, thinly sliced (3½ cups)
1 cup tomato paste
⅔ cup red wine vinegar
1 cup chopped pitted Sicilian olives in brine
½ cup capers in brine, drained
½ cup sugar
2 teaspoons unsweetened cocoa powder
Fine sea salt and coarsely ground black pepper
    to taste

Place the eggplant in a colander, sprinkle with coarse salt, and let sweat in the sink or on a plate for 1 hour. Rinse and dry well.

In a small saucepan, bring the water to a boil. Add the celery and cook for 3 to 4 minutes. Drain the celery, reserving the water, and set aside.

In a large skillet, heat ¾ cup peanut oil. Add half the eggplant and fry, stirring occasionally, until softened and lightly browned, 12 to 15 minutes. Remove to brown paper to drain. Repeat with the remaining eggplant, adding more peanut oil as necessary. Drain off the oil.

In the same frying pan, heat the olive oil over medium-high heat. Add the onions and sauté until soft, about 10 minutes. Lower the heat to medium, add the tomato paste, the reserved celery water, the vinegar, olives, capers, sugar, and cocoa and mix well. Let simmer for about 5 minutes. Add the eggplant and celery, stir well, and let simmer for about 10 minutes. Add the salt and pepper.

Spoon the caponata into clean jars, cap, and refrigerate or freeze. (If freezing, be sure to allow room for expansion in the jars.) Serve at room temperature.

A Baker's Glossary

■

Alcohol: A byproduct of the yeast fermentation process.

Carbon dioxide: A gas given off by the fermentation process caused by the expansion of multiplying yeast cells as they feed on the sugar and starches in the dough.

Crumb: The interior grain or texture of bread; it can be coarse, fine, loose, or tight. Factors determining texture include whether a slack, wet dough using more water is made that produces more holes, and an open texture or a firmer dough is made using less water and producing a closed, even textured crumb. Other factors determining the type of crumb include how long the dough was kneaded to develop the gluten and the amount of yeast used.

Crust: The exterior of bread; it can be crisp and chewy or soft and shiny. Crisp crusts are obtained with straight water, yeast, flour, and salt mixed doughs that are misted with water just after the risen dough is put into the oven to bake. The creation of steam allows for a crisp crust to develop. Breads made from sweet doughs enriched with eggs, butter, milk, and sugar had softer crusts.

Fermentation: The activity of dough once it is combined with water, yeast, and flour and left to rise.

Gluten: Protein in flour that forms strands when a liquid is added. It is an elastic substance that traps carbon dioxide gas and causes the dough to rise. Without gluten, it would be impossible to stretch dough.

Knead: To work a mass of dough on a surface by hand in order to stretch the dough, make it more elastic and smooth, and evenly distribute the gases and yeast cells in the dough.

Mixing: The process of combining water, yeast, and flour to make a dough.

Proof: To allow yeast and water to get chalky, cloudy, or foamy looking before adding the flour.

Punch down: To deflate risen dough gently with your fists in order to distribute the gases and gluten.

Rest: To allow the dough to sit between kneadings in order to relax the gluten and to allow the flour in the dough to absorb the water, making it easier to roll and work by hand.

Rise: The action of the multiplication of yeast cells and the formation of carbon dioxide that allows the prepared dough to increase in volume.

Score: To make several slashes with a razor, scissors, or lame in risen bread before it goes into the oven.

Sponge: A mixture of water, yeast, and flour allowed to double or even triple in volume before being added to additional water, yeast, and flour to give more strength to dough and a deeper flavor.

Yeast: Single cell fungi that feed on sugar and starches and promote alcoholic fermentation.

Mail-Order Sources

Anichini, Inc.
Rte. 110
Tunbridge, Vermont 05077
800–553–5309
Italian linens, including kitchen towels,
tablecloths, napkins, runners

Bridge Kitchenware
214 East 52nd Street
New York, New York 10022
212–688–4220
Baking pans, cookie sheets; catalogue

Chef's Catalogue
3215 Commercial Avenue
Northbrook, Illinois 60062–1900
800–338–3232
Baking equipment, heavy-duty electric mixers,
professional-quality stainless steel measuring cups
and spoons

Dairy Fresh Candies
57 Salem Street
Boston, Massachusetts 02113
800–336–5536
Citron, lemon and orange zests,
chocolate, dried fruits and nuts;
catalogue

Draeger's
P.O. Box C
Menlo Park, California 94026
800–642–9463
Baking supplies, dishes, and cookware

Fante's
1006 South 9th Street
Philadelphia, Pennsylvania 19147
800–878–5557
Italian cooking and baking equipment, including
parchment paper, pastry bags and tips, biscuit
cutters; catalogue

Gallucci's Italian Foods
6610 Euclid Avenue
Cleveland, Ohio 44103
216-881-0045
A complete Italian grocery store and on-premise
bakery shop. Cheeses, olives, olive oil, pasta, herbs,
spices, cured meats, vinegars, wines, imported
Mediterranean sea salt; catalogue

King Arthur Flour Baker's Catalogue
P.O. Box 1010
Norwich, Vermont 05055
800–827–6836
Unbleached flours, dried yeast, curried lemon and
orange peel, baking chocolate, baking supplies
www.kingarthurflour.com

Kitchen Etc.
32 Industrial Drive
Exeter, New Hampshire 03833
800–232–4070
Complete line of kitchenware and bakeware,
parchment paper, perforated pizza pans, charlotte
molds, springform pans; catalogue

Lamalle Kitchenware
36 West 25th Street
New York, New York 10010
All kinds of cooking and baking equipment;
catalogue

Lochhead Vanilla Company
3 Enfield Road
Saint Louis, Missouri 63132
314–772–2124
Pure extracts; catalogue

Melissa's
P.O. Box 21127
Los Angeles, California 90021
800–588–0151
Specialty foods and spices, including fresh and
dried fruits, dried tomatoes in olive oil, dried
porcini mushrooms, dried, hot peppers; catalogue

Joe Pace and Son Grocer
42 Cross Street
Boston, Massachusetts 02113
Italian products—cured meats, cheeses, olives,
olive oils, Amaretti cookies; catalogue

Previn Incorporated
2044 Rittenhouse Square
Philadelphia, Pennsylvania 19103
215–985–1996
Bakeware, including brioche molds, cream-horn
forms, baking sheets

Sur La Table
84 Pine Street
Pike Place Farmer's Market
Seattle, Washington 98101
800–243–0852
Complete line of baking equipment, including
cannoli and cream-horn forms, rolling pins,
biscuit cutters; catalogue

Zabar's
2245 Broadway
New York, New York 10024
212–787–2000
Kitchenware and gourmet food products;
catalogue

Index

◼

Numbers in italics refer to photographs.

M

madre, for Nonna's sponge dough, 59
mango:
  and dried cherry pie, *114*, 115
  stained-glass tomato tart, *62*, 63–64
Marsala:
  bread pudding, *120*, 121
  plum kuchen, *108*, 109
  twisted bread ring with prunes and (ciambella), *94*, 95–96
mashed potatoes, lemony, 132
measuring:
  cups, 5
  spoons, 5
meat and cheese filling, for Calabrian pitta, 69–70, *70*
milk, lowfat vs. whole, for baking, 2, 85
mini brioche, baker's dozen, 93
mixer, heavy-duty stand, 5
  Nonna's sponge dough in, 61
  simply sweet dough in, 87–88
  straight dough in, 20, 21
mixing dough, *10, 11, 12*
molasses, 2
  raisin bread, country, 72–73
mold, charlotte, 4–5, 91
mozzarella cheese:
  Calabrian pitta, *68*, 69–70
  roasted vegetable calzones, 82–83
mozzarella cheese, fresh:
  grilled pizza, *76, 77*
  pizza quattro stagioni (four seasons pizza), 43–44, *44*
muffins, English, *102*, 103
mushroom pizza, 80
mushrooms (rolls), *40*, 41
mustard, spicy, 137

N

Nonna's sponge dough, 59–61
  braided poppy seed bread, 65

bread basket bread, *66*, 67
Calabrian pitta, *68*, 69–70
caponata tartlets, 74–75
country raisin molasses bread, 72–73
focaccine with herbs, 71
grilled pizza, *76, 77*
mushroom pizza, 80
pumpkin seed, sage, and pancetta bread, *78, 79*
roasted vegetable calzones, 82–83
stained-glass tomato tart, *62*, 63–64
Swiss chard pizza, 81
Nonna's tomato pizzette, *46*, 47
nuts:
  storing, 3
  toasting, 3

O

olive oil, 3
  baking spray, 1, 13
  dried tomatoes in, 138
olives:
  Calabrian pitta, *68*, 69–70
  caponata, 140
  grilled pizza, *76, 77*
  pizza quattro stagioni (four seasons pizza), 43–44, *44*
  sailor-style bread salad, *124, 125*
  Swiss chard pizza, 81
  tangy tomato logs, *32, 33*
onions, red:
  mushroom pizza, 80
  panzanella (bread salad), 126
  potato, and spring mustard pizza, 45
orange peel, candied, 135
  Sunday coffee cake, 107
orange zest:
  bread pudding, *120*, 121
  ciambella (twisted bread ring with prunes and Marsala), *94*, 95–96
  freezing, 4

iris (Sicilian ricotta and chocolate pies), 37–39, *38*
poppy seed pretzels, 99–100

P

Palermo, 37
pancetta, sage, and pumpkin seed bread, *78, 79*
pane:
  casereccio (homemade bread), 22
  gnocchi di (bread gnocchi), 123
Panificio Melli, 41
pans:
  jelly-roll, 5
  pizza, 5, 27
panzanella (bread salad), 126
parchment paper, 5
Parmigiano-Reggiano cheese:
  focaccine with herbs, 71
  gnocchi di pane (bread gnocchi), 123
  grated pasta (*pasta grattata*), 128
  mushroom pizza, 80
pasta grattata (grated pasta), 128
pastry:
  brushes, 5
  cream, for Fat Tuesday donuts, 105
  wheel, 5
Pecorino Romano cheese, 23
  soup with bread under it, 131
  speckled spinach bread, 52–53
peel, candied orange, 135
peppers:
  Calabrian pitta, *68*, 69–70
  fennel and pork calzones, *47*, 48
  focaccia doppia (double-crusted focaccia), 27–28, *29*
  Italian country chicken pie, *34*, 35–36
  panzanella (bread salad), 126
  pizza quattro stagioni (four seasons pizza), 43–44, *44*
  roasted vegetable calzones, 82–83

Perugia, 95
Piazza del Pero, 80
pie:
  Italian country chicken, *34, 35–36*
  mango and dried cherry, *114,* 115
  scallop and haddock, 51–52
pies, Sicilian ricotta and chocolate (iris), 37–39, *38*
pitta, Calabrian, *68,* 69–70
pizza:
  fritta (fried dough), 30
  grilled, *76, 77*
  pans, 5
  quattro stagioni (four seasons pizza), 43–44, *44*
  spicy mustard, potato, and red onion, 45
  Swiss chard, 81
pizzette, Nonna's tomato, *46,* 47
plastic wrap, 5
plum kuchen, *108,* 109
poppy seed:
  bread, braided, 65
  pretzels, 99–100
porcini mushrooms, 80
pork:
  Calabrian pitta, *68,* 69–70
  and fennel calzones, *48, 49*
  grissini rustici (country breadsticks), *24, 25, 26*
  pumpkin seed, sage, and pancetta bread, *78, 79*
  spinach, and Fontina tart, spring, 56
portobello mushroom pizza, 80
potato:
  lemony mashed, 132
  spicy mustard, and red onion pizza, 45
  water, for Nonna's sponge dough, 57, 58
pretzels, poppy seed, 99–100

prosciutto:
  Calabrian pitta, *68,* 69–70
  grissini rustici (country breadsticks), *24,* 25, *26*
  spinach, and Fontina tart, spring, 56
provolone, aged:
  grissini rustici (country breadsticks), *24,* 25, *26*
  Swiss chard pizza, 81
prunes, twisted bread ring with Marsala and (ciambella), *94,* 95–96
pudding, bread, *120,* 121
pumpkin seed, sage, and pancetta bread, *78, 79*

Q

quattro stagioni pizza (four seasons pizza), 43–44, *44*
quick tomato sauce, 138

R

raisin:
  Louisa's bread stuffing, 127
  molasses bread, country, 72–*73*
red onion:
  mushroom pizza, 80
  panzanella (bread salad), 126
  potato, and spicy mustard pizza, 45
red peppers:
  Calabrian pitta, *68,* 69–70
  fennel and pork calzones, *47,* 48
  focaccia doppia (double–crusted focaccia), 27–28, *29*
  Italian country chicken pie, *34,* 35–36
  panzanella (bread salad), 126
  pizza quattro stagioni (four seasons pizza), 43–44, *44*
  roasted vegetable calzones, 82–83
Red Star yeast, 3

Reggio Emilia, 41
ricotta and chocolate pies, Sicilian (iris), 37–39, *38*
ring, twisted bread, with prunes and Marsala (ciambella), *94,* 95–96
roasted vegetable calzones, 82–83
rolling pins, 6
rolls:
  baker's dozen mini brioche, 93
  mushrooms, *40,* 41
  Tuscan rosemary and currant, 42
rosemary:
  and currant rolls, Tuscan, 42
  focaccia doppia (double-crusted focaccia), 27–28, *29*

S

sage, pumpkin seed, and pancetta bread, *78, 79*
sailor-style bread salad, *124,* 125
salad:
  bread (panzanella), 126
  sailor-style bread, *124,* 125
salt, 3
Sandri's pasticcerìa, 95
sauce, quick tomato, 138
scale, digital, 6
scallop and haddock pie, 51–52
scoring dough, 16
sea salt, 3
seeds, storing, 3
sesame:
  bread, braided, 23
  seeds, storing, 3
shaped breads:
  mushrooms, *40,* 41
  vendemmia bread, 54–55
shaping dough, 15, *17, 18*
Sicilian:
  ice cream cones, *110,* 111
  ricotta and chocolate pies (iris), 37–39, *38*
Sicily, xvii, 37, 140